SELECTION OF MODELS BY FORECASTING INTERVALS

A. H. Q. M. MERKIES

SELECTION OF MODELS BY FORECASTING INTERVALS

D. REIDEL PUBLISHING COMPANY

DORDRECHT-HOLLAND / BOSTON-U.S.A.

MODELKEUZE VIA VOORSPELLINGSINTERVALLEN
First published in 1972 by Academic Service, Amsterdam
Translated from the Dutch by M. van Holten-de Wolff

Library of Congress Catalog Card Number 73-83565

ISBN 90 277 0342 6

Published by D. Reidel Publishing Company,
P.O. Box 17, Dordrecht, Holland

Sold and distributed in the U.S.A., Canada, and Mexico
by D. Reidel Publishing Company, Inc.
306 Dartmouth Street, Boston,
Mass. 02116, U.S.A.

Printed in The Netherlands by D. Reidel, Dordrecht

TABLE OF CONTENTS

PREFACE

This book appeared as a Ph.D. thesis for the University of Amsterdam.

I hope it will be of interest to others. I owe grateful thanks to many people who – consciously or not – have given me their support. This refers mainly to Prof. Dr. J. S. Cramer who not only as director of the Instituut voor Actuariaat en Econometrie gave me ample time and all the research facilities needed but who also represented everything one may expect from a promoter. I also thank Prof. Dr. J. Koerts of the Netherlands School of Economics who read the manuscript and gave many helpful comments.

Many others have made stimulating remarks. Among them A. F. de Vos and F. A. G. den Butter also gave assistance in drawing up computer programs. Earlier this was done by F. X. Portier, then at the C.P.B. at The Hague. The graphs were drawn by H. van Oortmerssen. The errors are mine.

Finally, I thank my wife for her patience and her help. It is to her and to our children that I dedicate this book.

CHAPTER I

INTRODUCTION

Ever since the augures and priestesses of Delphi gave their vision on future events, little has changed in the need of man to know his future. In our time we try to endow our forecasts with more cogency by basing them on quantitative data on the developments in the past. Modern econometric forecasts are nothing but a logical continuation of the sketched lines from the past.

Since the thirties by building macro-economic models an important step forward was made in the direction of a consistent diagnosis of macro-economic developments. However, now that more recently fast-working computers do no longer obstruct the comparison of various kinds of alternative models, a new vacuum has been created. The diagnosis of the past appears not to be so simple that the making of a forecast would only require the extension of *one* single line of development. As a rule one escapes from this impasse by giving a certain model some preference, on whatever grounds, so that one gets the original situation of one single model, after all. A disadvantage here is that it is often not clear why exactly this model was chosen. Someone else, on the basis of the same data, would mostly have made a different choice, sometimes with considerable discrepancies in forecasting results. The choice of the most suitable linear model for macro-economic forecasts is the subject of this book.

First in Chapter II the basic assumption is presented that not just *one* model presents itself as the only correct one to describe the developments in the past, so that forecasting is in fact a problem of selecting the most proper model for the situation at hand. In this book this will be interpreted as the searching for the linear model with the smallest 95% forecasting interval. This will be further elaborated in Chapter III.

Not all linear models are admitted to the selection. For, if a model does not give an adequate description of the development in the past, such a model will be eliminated. This is dealt with in Chapter IV, in which it is also indicated how a certain efficiency in selecting may be achieved.

In Chapter V a few points of the theory are illustrated by way of a forecast of the export surplus of the Netherlands. Although the few examples are only meant to be a partial illustration of the text, yet a forecasting formula is obtained which could have been able to keep up the competition with the forecasts that were published in the sixties by the Dutch Central Planning Bureau.

CHAPTER II

FORECASTING AS A SELECTION PROBLEM

The first little monkey kept his little
hands over his eyes so tight:
"When I don't see anything wrong
I'll see everything that's right".

(Nursery rhyme)

2.1. Introduction

In this chapter the forecasting of economic magnitudes is presented as a choice between alternative views on the future development. The manner in which the forecast is finally calculated from the available data is called forecasting procedure. The definitions are enumerated in Section 2.2. The existence of alternative views on the future is dealt with in Section 2.3 under the heading 'Models'. In Section 2.4 a few words are devoted to the existing practice of forecasting. Finally Section 2.5 gives a survey of the selection problem.

2.2. Definitions

This book deals with the forecasting of quantitatively measurable economic variables. The values that are adopted at the moment t by the m magnitudes that are to be forecasted – *the process variables* – form the components of the columnvector $\mathbf{y}_t$.[1] This vector is stochastic, i.e. it should be considered as a drawing from a population with all possible values that y_t could have adopted.[2] The forecast of $\mathbf{y}_{t+\tau}$ at the moment t is indicated by $\hat{\mathbf{y}}_{t+\tau}$. The quality of the forecast is evaluated by way of the forecasting error $\mathbf{e}_{t+\tau}=\hat{\mathbf{y}}_{t+\tau}-\mathbf{y}_{t+\tau}$. The interval t, $t+\tau$ is called the *term of the forecasting*. When the term is not important we write briefly $\hat{\mathbf{y}}_\tau$ respectively $\mathbf{e}_\tau$ or, also $\hat{\mathbf{y}}_t$ respectively $\mathbf{e}_t$, providing the latter do not lead to misunderstandings. The moments for which a forecast is made will be referred to by *forecasting period*.

Only forecasts that are based on measurements in the past will be admitted. These measurements take place at discrete moments. Not only observations of $\mathbf{y}_t$ are admitted, but also those of other variables. The values that are adopted by the latter at the moment t together form the columnvector X_t with length k. The T respectively P observations of $\mathbf{y}_t$ and X_t may be combined in the matrices

$$Y = [y_{t_1} \; y_{t_2} \; \cdots \; y_{t_T}]$$

and

$$X' = [X_{t'_1} \; X_{t'_2} \; \cdots \; X_{t'_P}].$$

The intervals t_1, t_T and t'_1, t'_P are the observation periods.

In this book observations without further indication refer to the period immediately prior to the moment at which the forecast is made, the so called *reference period*. Therefore the indices t_i and t'_i run from $t-T$ to t, so

$$Y = [y_{t-T} \; y_{t-T+1} \; \cdots \; y_{t-1}]$$

and

$$X' = [X_{t-T} \; X_{t-T+1} \; \cdots \; X_{t-1}].$$

So here the observation period and the reference period coincide. The way in which $\hat{y}_t$ is calculated from Y and X is called a *forecasting procedure* or *forecasting scheme*.

We shall only discuss linear forecasting procedures. All of these satisfy

$$\hat{y}_t = A_1 y_{t-1} + \cdots + A_T y_{t-T} + B_1 X_{t-1} + \cdots + B_P X_{t-T} \qquad (2.1)$$

in which A_i and B_j are matrices of the order $(m \times m)$ respectively $(m \times k)$.

We shall mainly restrict ourselves to forecasting terms of 1 year and to estimated coefficients so that, as a rule, only the coefficients A_i and B_j and $\hat{y}_t$ are bold-face.

The restriction to *linear* forecasting procedures is related to the fact that we only introduce linear models and normally distributed disturbances.[3]

2.3. Models

2.3.1

Given the forecasting procedure the course of $\mathbf{e}_t$ is determined by the course of X_t and $\mathbf{y}_t$. Since y_t is only known for $t = t-T, \ldots t-1$, but not for the moment τ that is to be forecasted, in order to choose a forecasting procedure wellgroundedly one should build up a conception about the general behaviour of $\mathbf{y}_t$, about the relation with its observations in the past y_{t-i} and about the connections with other variables. This complex of ideas is called a *model.* Bertels and Nauta (1969) distinguish between a material model – the set of notions – and the formal model – the mathematical or mathematical-statistical description of it. It will be clear that evaluation of $\mathbf{e}_t$ demands a formal model.

If only one single model exists, one obviously links the forecasting procedure with it. It remains even to be seen whether it is to the point to give a name of its own (forecasting procedure) to the way the model is used for forecasts. However, in the following it will be made clear that there are more views on the future development. Yet, it is assumed that only one forecast is desired. This one forecast is computed with the help of the chosen forecasting procedure.

2.3.2

A model is in essence an aprioristic interpretation of reality. Since it can never be proved that one special interpretation is the right one, more views on the development are possible, in principle. Yet we assume all the time that we live in a logical and continuous world. Therefore models that are in conflict with this basic notion are not admitted. For the rest, we shall not go into the theoretical requirements a model must satisfy, such as requirements of proper dimension, of stability, etc. However, it must be stated explicitly that these requirements apply only to the forecasting period and the observation- or reference period.[4] So, theories that lead to nonsensical inferences if they are used outside the said periods are yet admitted in the limited frame.

Due to the requirement of continuity the model must also be applicable to the *reference period.* It must be determined by means of observations to what extent this is true. For this purpose the models are formulated again in measured equivalents of model variables. One does not pretend to give a fully deterministic description of reality this way. Only headlines are being indicated. It is assumed that the errors of definition and measurement as well as the not mentioned factors that determine the development in a certain period, can be combined in a stochastic variable. We call it a stochastic model.

The introduction of stochastic models implies the possibility to have alternative interpretations of the general development. The data on the reference period form, after all, only a sample. And the latter has an acceptable value for different assumptions of the population. However, of some populations it can be said that the sample is not likely to have been drawn from it. This should always be checked. If it is not possible to do so, e.g. because only part of the model is known or because the number of observations is insufficient, the model is not testable. We shall not admit such models, neither those that appear to be too unlikely on account of a statistical test. A model that satisfies all said theoretical and empirical requirements is called *admitted.*

In econometrics a distinction is often made between *model* and *structure*. The first gives a general description of the relations between the examined variables, whereas a structure is the form the model adopts when all relations have been specified.[5] For linear models this means that a model indicates which variables get a coefficient different from zero, while in the structure a specific value is assigned to these coefficients. Econometrics has mainly concerned itself with the question how the 'true' structure is to be found amidst the set of structures that the model consists of. According to Christ (1966, p. 299) there are 'two kinds of gaps here'. The first is connected with 'limitations of the quantity and variety of the data used', the second 'with the restrictiveness of the model'. Extension of the sample will usually reduce the first 'gap', the second puts restrictions on the formulation of the model. The model must permit *identification* of the 'true' structure. It is now a crucial question whether the 'true' structure may be identified at all. According to Liu (1960) this is not possible for the macroeconomic structure of an economy. In other words, not a single macroeconomic model with a sufficient number of zero coefficients can be specified. As it is, a model is only an approximation to reality, and in this light a choice of a sufficient number of zero coefficients seems to be justified. However, the inference is that one should not restrict oneself to one single choice of zero coefficients. In other words one should proceed from more than one admitted model.

Various arguments may be given for the proposition that several admitted models can exist side by side. The arguments are the following:

(1) The behaviour of economic subjects is ruled by a multitude of important and less important determining factors. By stressing different dominating determining factors every time, and combining the remaining ones in a disturbance, alternative descriptions are obtained. For each

observation of the discussed behaviour the disturbance is regarded as a drawing from a probability distribution. With another choice of explanatory factors one has sometimes to assign other characteristics to the probability distribution, but it is often not *a priori* unacceptable to assume that the same characteristics occur in different alternatives.

N.B. It is especially important to investigate to what extent the determining factors are mutually independent. If they are not, it is not possible to incorporate a number of them in the disturbance without affecting the basic assumptions of the classical regression model, notably the assumption that the explanatory variable and the disturbance are uncorrelated[6].

As far as macro-relations are concerned, we should add to this that the way in which the aggregation took place (with reference to persons, districts, firms etc. in all kinds of variations) will be decisive for the choice of the explanatory variables. Often, a determining factor that has been stated explicitly in each of the relations that are to be aggregated, will also be mentioned in the aggregated relation, whereas non-common factors end up in the disturbance. The common factor changes with the way of aggregating. E.g. buyers of a similar nature can be taken together (e.g. government bodies or private firms) or one may aggregate over commodities. Finally it should be added that each commodity and every person is ultimately so unique qua character, time and place, that a non-aggregated relation is hard to imagine.

(2) It is often not possible to define the determining factors of a certain behaviour so explicitly that they fall in with actually measured variables or a combination of them. This implies that often available observations must be used as 'proxies' of the intended variable. This is especially true when some kind of expectation enters the equation as an explanatory variable.

(3) It is not possible to indicate on theoretical grounds which mathematical function is the most suitable for the description of a behaviour. Naturally, the simplest possible functions are preferable, but, even when one is limited to linear relations, the choice is still wide since the variables may be all kinds of transformations of observed magnitudes, such as linear in logarithms, growth percentages, reciprocals, squares, etc.

2.3.3

The above arguments indicate that it is not to the point to speak of the 'true' structure, but rather of admitted descriptions only. Since it is not very useful, with the existence of several admitted models to distinguish between structure and model, we shall only speak of models. To restrict the framework of the problem from now on only linear stochastic models are admitted with the annotation that linear models with transformed endogeneous variables are only admitted if the transformation(s) must be forecasted[7]. To be sure, this does not do justice to the above mentioned argument 3, but the analysis given here is merely a first start.

All admitted models fit into the relation

$$\mathbf{w}_t = \mathscr{A}_0\mathbf{w}_t + \mathscr{A}_1\mathbf{w}_{t-1} + \cdots + \mathscr{A}_R\mathbf{w}_{t-R} + \\ + \mathscr{B}_0 z_t + \mathscr{B}_1 z_{t-1} + \cdots + \mathscr{B}_N z_{t-N} + \mathbf{u}_t^* . \tag{2.2}$$

In this $\mathbf{w}_t$ is a vector with G endogeneous variables, z_t a nonstochastic vector with L exogeneous variables and $\mathscr{A}_i$ and $\mathscr{B}_j$ matrices of the order $G \times G$ respectively $G \times L$. $\mathbf{u}_t^*$ is a random drawing from a G-variate normal distribution with expectation 0 and variance-covariance matrix Φ, briefly written as $\mathbf{u}_t^* \cong N[0, \Phi]$.

The relation between (2.1) and (2.2) will further be discussed in Section 2.5. It is already clear that $G \geqslant m$, i.e. that the model must include at least the m variables that are to be forecasted. It will appear later on that in the line of thought of this book the model need not be larger indeed, so $G = m$[8].

A number of all models that are described by (2.2) are not admitted on theoretical or empirical grounds. However, a very large number of models that satisfy the requirements remains. This is mostly caused by the large number of variables that can occur in z. It cannot be determined without further analysis what variables we have here. It depends on scientific insight, imaginative faculty, availability of data, etc. So the set of models can be enlarged again and again. On the other hand, restrictions will also reduce the set because of new theoretical views or because some models give results that deviate significantly from the new data.

2.4. The practice of forecasting

2.4.1

In the practice of forecasting there are two schools. For reasons of convenience we shall refer to their techniques as the 'econometric' and 'process control' forecasting procedure (exponential smoothing), or as the procedure of 'econometricians' as opposed to the one of the 'controllers'. The first method is indeed mainly used by economists in generating macro-economic forecasts, the second originates from the process control and has been transposed by Wiener (1949) to the prediction of time series. It is mainly used as part of predictions dealing with business economics. There is a number of differences that are especially based on pragmatic grounds.

What the controllers want is in the first place to set up fast and simple algorithms that enable them to forecast a large number of separate variables. Accordingly, unlike the 'econometricians', they distinguish explicitly between model and forecasting procedure [9]. They neither analyse nor look for causal relationships. Yet, one realises that the usefulness of the procedure depends on the kind of variable that is to be forecasted. Consequently it is examined how the procedures react to various models. However, the model concept is little developed with controllers. The actions of their procedures are only tested on models with one variable, which is an explicit function of time, supplemented by a disturbance that may or may not be autocorrelated. The procedures involved make only use of the process variables themselves. I.e. only those variations of (2.1) for which A_i=diagonal and $B_j=0$ hold. The results of their procedures are often called 'forecasts' in contrast with 'predictions' which (also) use exogeneous variables. However, this nomenclature has been used the other way round as well.[10] The using or not using other variables than those that are to be forecasted forms, in fact, only one aspect of the difference between the econometric school and that of the controllers. Another difference is that 'controllers' explicitly use forecasting errors. Often the forecasting procedure can also be written as a function of the committed forecasting error(s). One expressly adjusts, and check-charts or control-charts are devised to follow the process, e.g. the Shewhart-chart or the Cusom-chart [11].

Econometricians also analyse forecasting errors [12] but these analyses have only indirect and lagged consequences for the forecasting procedure. The latter is only revised from time to time, if the analyses point to a bad forecast performance in certain situations or for some variables. With the analyses one distinguishes between 'conditional' and 'unconditional' forecasts. The 'condition' refers to the correctness of the information that is to be put in the forecasting procedure. Clearly, this is of less importance to the 'controllers' because with them data refer only to observations of previous periods, and, moreover, their data are often more promptly available. In the 'econometric' forecasts many inputdata are used that relate to the future and that are estimated for that purpose. This estimation takes also place on the basis of information from the past, but this information is not always of a quantitative nature, such as announced changes in the law, declarations of Cabinet ministers, or trade union leaders, etc. And often the information is indeed quantitative but the method has not yet been formalised, so that the outsider cannot verify the value of the exogeneous variables with the basic information, e.g. granted licenses, changes of rates, etc. Finally, the values of the exogeneous variables are often attuned to the views of other forecasters, (OECD, ECE, research departments of banks and ministries, etc.), perhaps not quantified.

It will be clear, that with a method that has only partly been formalised, the forecasting *procedure* can only be evaluated on the basis of the actual course of the forecasting error. The analyses of suchlike 'unconditional forecasts' evaluate the complex of forecasting institution *and* forecasting method employed. They must be considered together. A comparison between the 'controllers'' forecast and the conditional forecasts of the 'econometricians' does not give a true picture, as in evaluating the conditional forecasts information is used that was, in fact, not available.

As regards the length of the reference period also there we have a difference between 'controllers' and 'econometricians'. The first explicitly state that the period is a choice variable.[13] Since discontinuities of the 'trendfractions' demand changes in policy and consequently must be discovered quickly, the forecasting procedure should not be insensitive to discontinuities of the 'trendfractions' and so, T in (2.1) must not be too large. On the other hand, when T is smaller, the variance of the forecasting error becomes larger *cet. par.* and the forecast, in this respect, worse. With 'econometricians' two trends can be noticed. Sometimes one likes to make one's model as general as possible and the length of the reference period is then only restricted by the data available.[14] Others explicitly restrict their model to a period with a specific structure, e.g. post-war,[15] or a recession period.[16]

2.4.2

The econometricians do not distinguish between forecasting procedure and model. This is understandable, from a historic point of view. Econometricians rather deal with the explanations of the developments than with a forecast. Their models are indeed pronounced to this. If one model would be preferable to all others, the results of a certain forecasting procedure would be easy to examine and, when a criterion of optimality has been formulated, the optimal forecasting procedure is often equally easy to find. We shall return to this when the criterion for optimality will have been formulated.[17]

However, more notable than the lacking of the distinction model – forecasting procedure is the fact that the existence of more than one model is seldom explicitly brought up for discussion, at least not in theory. Anyway, in my opinion this is insufficiently taken into account. Sometimes the constructed models are regarded as excerpts from a larger model. The various theories are then complementing explanations. Allen (1967, p. 57) remarks e.g.:

> Finally the factors mentioned may well be interrelated; certainly, we do not have to decide to include one at the expense of others. The investment function may best appear in several variables.

Sandee (1966, p. 480) says about this:

> And if theory teaches him – the econometrician – that the rate of interest influences the investments in a negative way, and if the testing on the historical course of investments provides no reason to reject that theory, then the rate of interest ought to be kept in the model[18] that is constructed by the economist. After all, it is possible for the rate of interest to reach an unprecedented level within this year and to influence the investments visibly for the first time.

These remarks suggest that the best thing would be to include *all* determinants of w_t. However, if one wishes to derive coefficients from the observations, or to include only *a priori* coefficients that can be tested, the number of variables that is to be included in the specification will be limited. Cramer (1969, §61) shows how from a deterministic view on the development of w_t namely

$$w = \phi(X_1, X_2, \ldots, X_h)$$

one arrives at a stochastic specification

$$\mathbf{w}_t = \beta_1 + \beta_1 X_{1t} + \cdots + \beta_t X_{kt} + \mathbf{U}_t$$

by neglecting a number of factors and including them in the disturbance $\mathbf{U}_t$. In the specification only the k variables, relevant for the analysis remain for which observations are available in the reference period and the cross partial derivatives with the r-k neglected variables of which are zero.[19] Those variables are relevant that are determined by the object of the analysis or variables, which do not have an intrinsic meaning but which contribute to the variance of the disturbance.

Within the frame of this work the question is important whether only one out of the $\binom{r}{k}$ variables varying inthe reference period satisfies the said conditions of observation and independence or whether there are more that do so. Cramer does not answer this question explicitly but his comment that the choice of the variables that are to be selected depends on the object of the investigation is only to the point if it is possible to use a different selection with a different object of investigation. Since the object of my book is: forecasting, all selections that satisfy the conditions may be included in principle.

Sometimes it is explicitly acknowledged that it is possible to have different specifications, yet one of them is considered to be the superior one. The question is then which variables should be included "And we often do not learn whether certain variables of perhaps secondary importance *should* be included or not."[20] A wrong choice of variables is called 'specification error'. If the existence of several correct models is assumed, a specification error should be differently defined, namely as the error made in the structuring of a model that, in reality, does not satisfy the assumptions made, especially not the assumptions of the regression model. The basic thought of this book is, indeed, not that incorrect specifications do not exist. Only: for $\mathbf{w}_t$ several models may be structured that satisfy the conditions of the regression model. It is a matter of testing to what extent incorrectness may come to light. This is dealt with in Section 4.3.

To this respect Theil (1965, p. 212) introduces apart from a so-called 'correct' model $\mathbf{y}=X_1\beta_1+\mathbf{u}_1$ with $E\mathbf{u}_1=0$ and $E\mathbf{u}_1\mathbf{u}_1'=\sigma^2 I$ a model with an 'incorrect' specification $\mathbf{y}=X_2\beta_2+\mathbf{u}_2$ and shows that the residual variance of the 'incorrect' specification – corrected for loss of degrees of freedom – is, on the average, not smaller than the one of the 'correct' specification. He argues that the corrected residual sum of squares is therefore a fair guiding principle to evaluate the correctness of the specification.

Theil's proof amounts practically to the following, since $E\mathbf{u}_1=0$ it holds that $E\mathbf{u}_1^2=\operatorname{var}\mathbf{u}_1=\operatorname{var}\mathbf{y}$, but since it has *not* been assumed that $E\mathbf{u}_2=0$, it holds that $E\mathbf{u}_2^2\geqq\operatorname{var}\mathbf{u}_2=\operatorname{var}\mathbf{y}$. If $\mathbf{s}_1^2$ and $\mathbf{s}_2^2$are unbiased estimators of respectively $E\mathbf{u}_1^2$ and $E\mathbf{u}_2^2$ then it follows that $E\mathbf{s}_1^2\leqq E\mathbf{s}_2^2$. If $X_1\beta_1=$ $=X_2\beta_2$ the symbol $=$ is relevant. Then, also in the second specification, $E\mathbf{u}_2=0$ and $E\mathbf{u}_2\mathbf{u}_2'=\sigma^2 I$.[21]

In the situation mentioned above specification 2 is in itself not incorrect. If one does not wish to consider certain determinants – regardless of their contribution to $E\mathbf{y}^2$ – and if one wishes to move them to the disturbance, the consequence is that $E\mathbf{u}_2^2$ and also the residual sum of squares will become larger. It does not follow that the model is incorrect. Specification 2 becomes only incorrect if one wrongly assumes $E\mathbf{u}_2=0$. However, as long as such an assumption has not been rejected by a test, both $E\mathbf{u}_1=0$ and $E\mathbf{u}_2=0$ are indeed possible. In fact, here the two are dealt with as being equivalent. Any *a priori* preference is subjective.

Theil advises, according to the quotation mentioned above, to let the quantity $\dfrac{\sum\hat{\mathbf{u}}_t^2}{T-k}$ decide in a case like that, because 'on the average' the correct assumption is then chosen. In my opinion this is an improper use of the term 'average'. One may not look upon the truth as a stochast. There is either only one correct model or there are several of them. In the second case the models remain equivalent. Then a criterion of efficiency must decide on the choice. In the first case one would only wish to choose the correct one. However, the latter is not known yet. It is possible then, within the limitations of the admitted hypotheses, to let a criterion of efficiency decide on the choice. Of course, Theil's criterion may also be used as a selection measure. However, it will appear in Chapter III that we propose to use a different measure for forecasting purposes.

It is possible that, due to an unfortunate sample, on the one hand correct models stay outside the set of admitted models, while on the other hand models that have not yet been proved to be incorrect are admitted. I agree with Wonnacott and Wonnacott (1970, p. 312) that the unjust admitting or leaving out of a variable has unfortunate consequences for the estimation of the variances and covariances of the other coefficients, but I consider them to be inevitable as long as one has not complete information at one's disposal. Considering all plausible alternatives is then in my opinion more important than searching for arguments to sustain the plausibility of an occasional 'sound prior specification'.

2.4.3

Although one starts in theory from one model, in practice this model must still be determined. With this a process comes in of selecting, once more defining and weighing against other possibilities. This has been described clearly by Sandee (1966, §3). So, the ultimate determination of the model or forecasting procedure is both subjective and obscure. Christ (1966, p. 8) comments:

> In this situation the economist has several choices. He can give up. The large number of pages remaining in this book suggest that this is not my recommendation. He can somehow choose one reasonable form of the equation, on grounds that are in part neither theoretical nor empirical and use it with relevant data to draw inferences.

The indistinctness of the choice can partly be explained by the fact that the purpose of the model that is to be constructed is stated insufficiently strictly. One wishes, on the basis of one model, both to analyse the developments in the past and to make forecasts, and moreover to examine the consequences of alternative policies. However, in order to obtain a better forecast one will often have to concentrate on other values of the explanatory variables than those used in the analysis.[22] I daresay this is most clear in relation to policy changes. These are indeed also forecasts, but with other assumptions. In the next chapter it will appear that in choosing between forecasting procedures we also consider the values of the exogeneous variables.

It may finally be remarked that, although one often gives a certain model priority over all others, yet one expresses the consequences of another choice of procedure.[23] See e.g. Kooyman and Merkies (1969).

2.5. The Framework of the Problem and its Restrictions

The fundamental starting point of this work is that a large number of models can be constructed with the help of which $\mathbf{y}_t$ can be described and, consequently, $\mathbf{e}_t$ can be evaluated. However, these models must satisfy a number of theoretical and empirical demands. In the concrete this means that it is required of the models that they fit in with the classical regression model, and also that they passed certain tests on the basis of the reference period. The character of the test is changed by the fundamental character of the startingpoint. One must indeed be very careful in the formulation of the alternative hypothesis. I shall revert to the question of the testing.[24]

After the testing a large number of possibilities remains. It is essential in my view that they are equivalent. It is true, one might arrange the models more or less on aprioristic grounds, (considerations of plausibility, non-quantifiable information) or one might introduce Bayesian methods, but these methods have not been broached here. It is my conviction namely, that it is recommendable first to have a given selection criterion decide upon the choice of the model and only afterwards to bring the said other considerations into the forecast. So, at a certain moment say H equivalent models remain that satisfy the requirements. We can number them $M_1, M_2, \ldots, M_H$. Apart from these models we can distinguish e.g. $K > H$ forecasting procedures. This leads to $S_1, S_2, \ldots, S_K$. See Table II.1.

TABLE II.1

Possible combinations of models and forecasting procedures; O = optimal for the given model

	M_1	M_2		M_H
S_1	O			
S_2		O		
S_H				O
S_K				

The 'econometric forecasting procedure' implies that, more or less arbitrarily, a model M_i is selected, the 'optimal' matching procedure of which is then searched for. For reasons of convenience, it has been assumed in the table that S_i is optimal for M_i. As argued, the optimal procedure can be derived immediately in many cases. This is indeed also dependent on the exact content of the selection criterion.[25] Sometimes only an asymptotically optimal procedure can be derived. In contrast to the above, one can also select a random S_j and investigate how it behaves when confronted with different models. This is the 'controllers'' approach. If one explicitly sets the complete set $\{M_i\}$ against $\{S_j\}$ still several possibilities remain. One might e.g. choose that procedure that scores highly with as many models as possible. This has the advantage that one need not give one's opinion on the choice of the model, and, consequently, is less dependent on the correctness of one's economic views. This procedure can then remain unchanged for a while. On the other hand, each S_j must then be confronted with each M_i, which is a very roundabout system. Moreover, the behaviour of $\mathbf{e}_t$ will sometimes be difficult to determine.

In this book I shall join the 'econometric' approach as much as possible. The difference, however, lies herein that there the set out of which model and forecasting procedure were chosen, is explicitly mentioned, as well as the criterion in accordance with which one particular forecasting procedure is ultimately preferred. The procedure that is optimal in accordance with the given criterion appears, as a rule, to be easy to determine and so, it is generally sufficient to compare the procedures of Table II.1 that are marked with an *O* with their respective models.

The procedure is then as follows. First a large number of models is collected. Then they are tested in one way or another. Every time the matching optimal procedure for an admitted model is searched for and afterwards that model and procedure are chosen that are optimal according to the chosen selection criterion.

The disadvantage of this method is that the optimal forecasting procedure for $\mathbf{y}_{t+\tau}$ may be dependent on t and τ so that one has to change to another procedure again and again. In practice one may of course adopt the rule that there will only be a change of procedures when the difference with the optimal one becomes important, or that the selection only takes place once per period.

I have the following in mind: Suppose $\mathbf{y}_\tau$ includes the most important economic variables. They must be forecasted for a large number of moments. As long as the technical problems connected with this have not been solved we restrict ourselves to forecastingperiods of *one* moment only. We select a forecastingprocedure on the ground of which the forecasts are generated. As we shall see in Chapter V the forecasts can easily be given as intervals. As time goes on new information becomes available. The original H models are tested again, unless they had been rejected on logical grounds. Some M_i that were earlier rejected because the underlying suppositions were not tenable on the basis of the information obtained till then, are yet accepted in the light of the new data. Others are rejected, either for the first time or once more. New models are added and also tested. From all models admitted so far the optimal one is again chosen and the new forecasts are given for the entire period. Apart from unfortunate coincidences[26] the forecast of $\mathbf{y}_\tau$ becomes more and more precise or more and more reliable.

Although in our set-up all models that satisfy the given theoretical and empirical demands have been admitted in principle, we have restricted ourselves in this book to models that can fit in with the classical regression model, without restrictions for the coefficients. This implies that we shall restrict ourselves to so-called reduced forms of non-identifiable models.[27] So, to what extent the introduction of restrictions may lead to smaller forecasting intervals is not stated here.

The argument continues as follows. In Chapter III the selection criterion is further developed. In Chapter IV it is indicated in what way the set of admitted models can be determined and what efficiency can be achieved in the selection. In Chapter V a number of aspects is illustrated with examples.

NOTES TO CHAPTER II

1 Depending on the length of the moment this definition covers currents as well as stock variables.

2 To stress this stochastic character the variables and vectors concerned are bold-face in imitation of the underlining suggested by Hemelrijk (1966).

3 See Subsections 2.3.3, 3.3.2 and 4.3.2.

4 Otherwise Somermeijer (1967).

5 Cf. Malinvaud (1964, p. 68).

6 Cramer (1969, p. 83).

7 See also Section 4.5.

8 See Subsection 3.2.2.

9 Van Winkel (1970).

10 Van Winkel (1970, p. 35).

11 Van Winkel (1970).

12 E.g. Van den Beld (1965).

13 Van Winkel (1970).

14 Klein and Goldberger (1955), Verdoorn and Van Eijk (1958) or Verdoorn and Post (1964).

[15] Van den Beld (1967), Van der Werf (1971).

[16] Duesenberry, Eckstein and Fromm (1960). Although with these authors the reference period does not coincide with a certain calendar period, they mention explicitly (p. 752) that their model can only be applied in a recession period.

[17] See Section 3.3.

[18] Mind the singular!

[19] One need not pay attention to the $h-r$ variables that are constant during the reference period.

[20] Christ (1966, p. 8). Italics mine.

[21] If $X_1\beta_1 = X_2\beta_2$ it holds that

$$E\mathbf{u}_2 = E(\mathbf{y} - X_2\beta_2) = E\mathbf{u}_1 = 0$$

and

$$\begin{aligned} \Omega = E\mathbf{u}_2\mathbf{u}'_2 &= E\mathbf{y}\mathbf{y}' - X_2\beta_2\beta'_2X'_2 \\ &= E\mathbf{y}\mathbf{y}' - X_1\beta_1\beta'_1X'_1 = E\mathbf{u}_1\mathbf{u}'_1 = \sigma^2 I. \end{aligned}$$

[22] See e.g. Sandee's comment on the interest rate, previously quoted.

[23] However, this comparing with alternative choices relates more often to other values of the exogeneous variables than to other values of the coefficients. With this one tries to escape the disadvantages of point-estimates for the exogeneous variables (see chapters 'Variances' in the yearly plans of the C.P.B. (Central Planning Bureau)).

[24] Cf. Section 4.3.

[25] Cf. Section 3.3.

[26] By chance the original intervals may turn out too small or the new ones too large. However, fortune's part will be gradually repelled.

[27] Indeed, in a model that can be identified there are restrictions on the reduced form coefficients.

CHAPTER III

THE CRITERION FOR SELECTION

3.1. Introduction

In Chapter II the criterion of optimality has already been mentioned several times. However, it has to be determined yet. The latter will be done in this chapter in the Sections 3.2 and 3.3 respectively, in the case in which the parameters of the models are given or in which they are estimated. In the same section the criterion is applied to determine the optimal number of equations. Afterwards, in Section 3.4 a criterion of selection is introduced which has the damage caused by the forecasting errors incorporated.

3.2. Models with parameters known

3.2.1. *The Criterion for Selection*

According to Wiener (1949, p. 13) the best forecast is:

> that which minimises the numerical measure of the difference between the actual future of a time series and its predicted future. This numerical measure should itself not be tied to an origin in time and should be a single quantity even though the difference which it measures is that between two functions. The numerical measure of an error we shall call its norm.

There are more criteria that satisfy the latter, as Wiener himself remarks. However, it seems most obvious to minimise the variance of the forecasting errors. This means that according to Wiener the optimal forecast of a scalar $\mathbf{y}_t$ implies that

$$E\mathbf{e}_t = 0 \tag{3.1}$$

$$\mathrm{Var}\,\mathbf{e}_t \quad \text{is a minimum}. \tag{3.2}$$

These criteria are in fact subjective. Cases occur in which the risk connected with an overestimation is larger than that of a forecast that is too low. However, if we wish to make a forecast that is as objective as possible, then the criterion of selection must be as general as possible. Especially for macro-economic forecasts the argument holds that these are used for several purposes and consequently have to be good in themselves.[1] For general purposes (3.2) together with (3.1) seems to be most appropriate. Anyway, they are the most usual ones. One also finds as a criterion[2]

$$E\mathbf{e}_t^2 = \operatorname{Var}\mathbf{e}_t + (E\mathbf{e}_t)^2 \quad \text{a minimum} \tag{3.3}$$

so without the requirement of unbiasedness which seems to be more attractive at first sight, because instead of 2 requirements – (3.1) and (3.2) – only 1 requirement is sufficient. For models with given parameters there is no objection against (3.3). The disadvantage of this criterion becomes only evident when the parameters of the model are to be estimated. For the optimal forecasting procedure following from (3.3) is dependent on the modelparameters.[3] This means that this procedure can only then be found if a sufficient number of restrictions has been imposed on the estimation of the parameters, either because a special distribution was chosen for the disturbance that is added to the model (e.g. a Poisson or log-normal distribution), or because the coefficients are given an *a priori* distribution as in a Bayesian analysis. As we limit ourselves to normal distributions, and from the next paragraph onwards we do not assume any previous knowledge of the parameters, in our set-up (3.2) in combination with (3.1) seems preferable to (3.3).

In macro-economic forecasts the vector $\hat{\mathbf{y}}_t$ usually contains more than 1 variable. This leads to a complication to this extent that one has instead of 1 number – $\operatorname{var}\mathbf{e}_t$ – set of numbers, namely the variance-covariance matrix of $\mathbf{e}_t$. Yet, to choose a model and the corresponding forecasting procedure also here 'a single quantity' is required. So the set of numbers of $E\mathbf{e}_t\mathbf{e}_t' = \Omega$ must first be reduced to one number only. This can be achieved by taking the determinant of Ω. $\operatorname{Det}\Omega$ defined by Wilks (1932) as the 'generalized variance' of the distribution of $\mathbf{e}_t$ fits in best as a criterion with the previously mentioned measure in the simple case. However, it should be added that this choice of the criterion is in fact just as arbitrary as with Wiener the choice of $E\mathbf{e}_t^2$ instead of e.g. $E\mathbf{e}_t^4$.

Two restrictions confine the use of $\det\Omega$ as a criterion for selection:

(1) If a forecast is needed of m magnitudes between which 1 or more than 1 exact linear relations exist, then Ω is singular and $\det\Omega$ cannot be used as a criterion. This situation is explicitly excluded here. This is hardly

a restriction. For, if there are k non-stochastic linear relationships between the m variables asked for, the comparison can take place on the basis of a minor of Ω of the order $m-k$. To be true, this rule is not unique, as on the basis of one $(m-k)$ minor model i, and on the basis of another minor model j can be chosen, but just as the aim of the forecast determines the m variables of the vector $\mathbf{y}_t$, this aim must also indicate which are the $m-k$ basic variables. From then on the prescribed procedure holds for $m-k$ instead of m.

(2) The units in which the elements of $\mathbf{e}_t$ have been expressed must be similar in the various models. For $\det\Omega$ is invariant against a choice of units no more than $\operatorname{var}\mathbf{e}_t$. However, if one chooses the same units in each model the selection is no longer dependent on the unit of measurement. For if in both models i and j the vector $\mathbf{y}_t$ and consequently also $\hat{\mathbf{y}}_t$ and $\mathbf{e}_t$ are measured in different units, for which we write $\mathbf{y}_t^*$, $\hat{\mathbf{y}}_t^*$ and $\mathbf{e}_t^*$ and if the transformationmatrix is M so that

$$\mathbf{y}_t^* = M\mathbf{y}_t \quad \text{and} \quad \mathbf{e}_t^* = M\mathbf{e}_t$$

then

$$\frac{\det\Omega_i^*}{\det\Omega_j^*} = \frac{\det(E\mathbf{e}_t^*\mathbf{e}_t^{*\prime})_i}{\det(E\mathbf{e}_t^*\mathbf{e}_t^{*\prime})_j} = \frac{\det M\Omega_i M'}{\det M\Omega_j M'} = \frac{\det\Omega_i}{\det\Omega_j}$$

holds because $\det M\Omega M' = (\det M)^2 \det\Omega$ for non-singular M and Ω. Summarizing it can be stated that the criterion for selection for the optimal forecast of $\mathbf{y}_t$ is

$$E\mathbf{e}_t = 0 \tag{3.4}$$

and

$$\det\Omega \quad \text{a minimum} \tag{3.5}$$

provided Ω is not singular and all forecasting procedures predict the same vector $\mathbf{y}_t$.

Instead of the above one may also start in the selection from the $(1-\alpha)\%$ confidence interval of $\mathbf{e}_t$ or of the normalized magnitude $\mathbf{e}_t'\Omega^{-1}\mathbf{e}_t$. In that case the procedure for the selection is as follows: Choose forecasting procedure S_j and model M_i in such a way that

$$E\mathbf{e}_t = 0 \tag{3.4}$$

and the volume V of the domain bounded by the ellipsoid

$$\mathbf{e}_t'\Omega^{-1}\mathbf{e}_t = c_\alpha^2 \tag{3.6}$$

is a minimum with given α.

For models with the same value of c_α and the same length of $\mathbf{e}_t$ selection according to (3.4) and (3.6) amounts to the same as selection according to (3.4) and (3.5). For, according to Cramér (1946, p. 114 and 120), the volume of the m-dimensional body V can be specified as

$$V = \frac{(\pi c_\alpha^2)^{m/2}\sqrt{\det \Omega}}{\Gamma\left(\frac{m}{2}+1\right)}. \tag{3.7}$$

With given m and c_α we have $V_i < V_j$ if $\det \Omega_i < \det \Omega_j$.

For models with the same value of m and different values of c_α one can also find a simple criterion, if (3.6) is standardised to

$$\mathbf{e}_t'(c_\alpha^2\Omega)^{-1}\,\mathbf{e}_t = 1$$

Then the selection takes place according to $\det c_\alpha^2\Omega$. This is the variable part of (3.7) with given m, for

$$V = \frac{\pi^{m/2}}{\Gamma\left(\frac{m}{2}+1\right)}\sqrt{c_\alpha^{2m}\det \Omega} = C_0\sqrt{\det c_\alpha^2\Omega}$$

in which C_0 is a constant that depends only on m.

In this way the general criterion for selection of models with known parameters can be formulated.

Summary 1

From the set of models with known parameters that model and corresponding procedure will be selected for which

$$\boxed{E\mathbf{e}_t = 0} \tag{3.4}$$

and

$$\boxed{\det c_\alpha^2\Omega \quad \text{is a minimum}} \tag{3.8}$$

provided Ω is not singular and $\mathbf{y}_t$ is in all models the same vector with length m.

3.2.2. *The Optimal Number of Equations of the Model*

The criterion for selection that was presented in the previous paragraph will now be applied to determine *the optimal number of equations* of the model. In doing so we start from (2.2) with given parameters $\mathscr{A}_i$, $\mathscr{B}_j$ and Ψ, but we restrict ourselves to forecasts that are computed on the basis of known magnitudes. In models with lagged endogeneous variables this implies a restriction to forecasting terms not longer than the shortest lag that occurs in the model.[4] In such cases the lagged values of $\mathbf{w}_t$ are known and consequently not stochastic. (2.2) can then be written as

$$\mathbf{w}_t = \mathscr{B}^* z_t^* + \mathbf{u}_t \tag{3.9}$$

in which

$$z_t^{*\prime} = [w_{t-1}', w_{t-2}', \ldots, w_{t-R}', z_t', z_{t-1}', \ldots, z_{t-N}']$$

and

$$\mathscr{B}^* = [I - \mathscr{A}_0]^{-1} [\mathscr{A}_1, \mathscr{A}_2, \ldots, \mathscr{A}_R, \mathscr{B}_0, \mathscr{B}_1, \ldots, \mathscr{B}_N].$$

Moreover

$$\mathbf{u}_t = (I - A)^{-1} \mathbf{u}_t^* \cong N(0, \Psi) \tag{3.10}$$

with Ψ of the order $G \times G$ and rank G.

As long as the parameters $\mathscr{B}^*$ are given, the best linear predictor of $\mathbf{w}_t$ is

$$\hat{w}_t = \mathscr{B}^* z_t^* . \tag{3.11}$$

Then

$$E\boldsymbol{\varepsilon}_t = E(\hat{w}_t - \mathbf{w}_t) = E\mathbf{u}_t = 0$$

and

$$\det E\boldsymbol{\varepsilon}_t\boldsymbol{\varepsilon}_t' = \det \Psi$$

We now have a starting-point to determine the *optimal number of equations* of the model. For, it has not yet been indicated what length $\mathbf{w}_t$ should have. It has merely been stated that to predict the m variables of $\mathbf{y}_t$ the vector $\mathbf{w}_t$ must have at least the length m. So $G \geqslant m$. It will be shown hereafter that m is also the maximum length with normally distributed $\boldsymbol{\varepsilon}_t$. So $G = m$.

For clearness' sake we distinguish:

Model G: The model incorporated in (3.9) and (3.10) $\mathbf{w}_t$ contains the endogeneous variables of the model divided into process variables $\mathbf{y}_t$ and the remaining ones $\mathbf{w}_t^0$. So

$$\mathbf{w}_t = \begin{bmatrix} \mathbf{y}_t \\ \mathbf{w}_t^0 \end{bmatrix}.$$

Model m: The submodel of $\mathbf{w}_t$ that only contains $\mathbf{y}_t$ so

$$\mathbf{y}_t = \mathscr{B}_1^* z_{1t}^* + \mathbf{u}_{1t} \tag{3.9.1}$$

and

$$\mathbf{u}_{1t} = N(0, \Omega). \tag{3.10.1}$$

The optimal forecasting procedure is here

$$\mathbf{y}_t = \mathscr{B}_1^* z_{1t}^*. \tag{3.11.1}$$

From (3.9), (3.10) and (3.11) follows

$$\boldsymbol{\varepsilon}_t = \hat{w}_t - \mathbf{w}_t = \mathbf{u}_t \cong N(0, \Psi).$$

Likewise

$$\mathbf{e}_t = \hat{y}_t - \mathbf{y}_t = \mathbf{u}_{1t} \cong N(0, \Omega).$$

According to Graybill (1961, p. 83) for normally distributed $\boldsymbol{\varepsilon}_t$ with expectation 0 and variance-covariance matrix Ψ the expression $\boldsymbol{\varepsilon}_t' B \boldsymbol{\varepsilon}_t$ is distributed as χ^2 (k) if and only if $A = B\Psi$ is idempotent with rank k. If $B = \Psi^{-1}$ we get $A = I$ with rank G. So the expression $\boldsymbol{\varepsilon}_t' \Psi^{-1} \boldsymbol{\varepsilon}_t$ is distributed as $\chi^2(G)$. For a given type I probability α the confidence interval $\boldsymbol{\varepsilon}_t' \Psi^{-1} \boldsymbol{\varepsilon}_t \leqslant \chi_\alpha^2$ can be derived by reading the values of χ^2 corresponding to the given α off the χ^2 table.

Likewise $\mathbf{e}_t' \Omega^{-1} \mathbf{e}_t$ is distributed as $\chi^2(m)$. The $(1-\alpha)\%$ confidence interval is $\mathbf{e}_t' \Omega^{-1} \mathbf{e}_t \leqslant \chi_\alpha^2(m)$.

Now consider the following experiment:

We choose a type I probability α and construct the $(1-\alpha)\%$ confidence intervals

$$\mathbf{e}_t' \Omega^{-1} \mathbf{e}_t \leqslant \chi_\alpha^2(m) \tag{3.12}$$

and

$$\boldsymbol{\varepsilon}_t' \Psi^{-1} \boldsymbol{\varepsilon}_t \leqslant \chi_\alpha^2(G) \tag{3.13}$$

We draw a sample from the G-dimensional normal distribution of $\boldsymbol{\varepsilon}_t$. That is

$$\varepsilon_t = \begin{bmatrix} \mathrm{e}_t \\ \varepsilon_t^0 \end{bmatrix} \tag{3.14}$$

If e_t from (3.14) satisfies (3.12) the elements $e_{1t}, e_{2t}, \ldots, e_{mt}$ are written down on list 1. If e_t does not satisfy (3.12) nothing is written down on list 1. Only the sequence number of the drawing is kept account of.

Subsequently $\boldsymbol{\varepsilon}_t$ is tested on (3.13). If $\boldsymbol{\varepsilon}_t$ from (3.14) satisfies (3.12) the elements of e_t are written down on list 2. The vector $\boldsymbol{\varepsilon}_t^0$ is neglected. If $\boldsymbol{\varepsilon}_t$ does not satisfy (3.13) only the sequence number of the drawing is kept record of.

The drawings are repeated. With a sufficiently large number of drawings it will appear that the number of vectors noted down on both lists is $(1-\alpha)\%$ of the number of drawings. However, the values that were written down on both pages are not the same. The values of e_t on list 1 are all in the interval (3.12), those of list 2 in the larger interval

$$\mathbf{e}_t' \Omega^{-1} \mathbf{e}_t \leqslant \chi_\alpha^2 (G) \tag{3.15}$$

This is the projection of (3.13) in the m dimensions of $\mathbf{e}_t$[5,6].

Proof Belonging to (3.15)

The values of $\mathbf{e}_t$ and the interval within which they are do not change when the vector $\boldsymbol{\varepsilon}_t$ is transformed in such a way that the forecasting errors of the irrelevant variables are orthogonal with respect to $\mathbf{e}_t$. This takes place as follows:

$$\Psi = \begin{bmatrix} \Psi_{11} & \Psi_{12} \\ \Psi_{21} & \Psi_{22} \end{bmatrix} \quad \text{in such a way that} \quad \Psi_{11} = \Omega .$$

Transform $\boldsymbol{\varepsilon}_t$ by way of $\boldsymbol{\eta}_t = P\boldsymbol{\varepsilon}_t$, in which

$$P = \begin{bmatrix} I & 0 \\ -\Psi_{21}\Psi_{11}^{-1} & I \end{bmatrix} \quad \text{with rank } G$$

so according to Anderson (1958, p. 19)

$$\boldsymbol{\eta}_t = \begin{bmatrix} \mathbf{e}_t \\ \boldsymbol{\eta}_t^0 \end{bmatrix} \cong N(0, P\Psi P') .$$

So we can form the $(1-\alpha)\%$ confidence interval

$$\boldsymbol{\eta}_t' [P\Psi P']^{-1} \boldsymbol{\eta}_t \leqslant \chi_\alpha^2 (G). \tag{3.16}$$

Since according to Anderson (1958, p. 24)

$$P\Psi P' = \begin{bmatrix} \Psi_{11} & 0 \\ 0 & \Psi_{22} - \Psi_{21}\Psi_{11}^{-1}\Psi_{12} \end{bmatrix} = \begin{bmatrix} \Omega & 0 \\ 0 & R \end{bmatrix}$$

we can write (3.16) as

$$\boldsymbol{\eta}_t' \begin{bmatrix} \Omega^{-1} & 0 \\ 0 & R^{-1} \end{bmatrix} \boldsymbol{\eta}_t \leqslant \chi_\alpha^2(G)$$

or

$$\mathbf{e}_t'\Omega^{-1}\mathbf{e}_t + \boldsymbol{\eta}_t^{0\prime}R^{-1}\boldsymbol{\eta}_t^0 \leqslant \chi_\alpha^2(G)$$

and as both Ω^{-1} as R^{-1} are positive definite the following equation holds, regardless of the value of $\boldsymbol{\eta}_t^0$

$$\mathbf{e}_t'\Omega^{-1}\mathbf{e}_t \leqslant \chi_\alpha^2(G)$$

So if $\mathbf{y}_t$ is predicted on the basis of model G then the corresponding confidence interval is (3.15) and it is (3.12) on the basis of model m. Since $\chi_\alpha^2(m) < \chi_\alpha^2(G)$ for all values of α the area of (3.12) is smaller than that of (3.15)

So extension of the model with $(G-m)$ stochastic variables can never reduce the forecasting interval as long as the magnitudes are normally distributed. On the other hand $\mathbf{w}_t$ must at least have the length m, if we are interested in m variables. Extension with non-stochastic variables is unnecessary as this will only result in a singular matrix Ψ, so that the restrictions will not be satisfied. As described, in that case one would have to make a selection on the basis of a minor of Ψ of the order m. One ends up with the same variance-covariance matrix as the one in the model with the m variables to be predicted.

3.3. Models with estimated variables

3.3.1

So far models with given expectation and given variance-covariance matrix have been discussed. However, in doing so one has not yet achieved a link with reality. So one would either have to test the given assumptions on the basis of the reference period or to estimate the parameters. The core of the distinction lies in the fact that the estimators of the parameters are stochastic and consequently possess a variance. These variances cause an enlargement of the confidence interval. So, with a selection according to (3.4) and (3.8) it would be better to start from models with given coefficients and, in order to achieve the required link with reality to test them with the observations of the reference period. However, one should bear in mind that the coefficients used can only then be considered to possess no variance if their values are independent of the observations. This is only the case when the choice between 2 or more possible coefficients takes place on purely theoretical grounds. As soon as empirical considerations are also taken into account, the choice of a coefficient is no longer independent of the observations. So, in general one may adopt two courses. Either in the whole set of models only one alternative is included for a certain coefficient – in that case the variance of that coefficient is 0 – or the parameters are regarded as unknowns and estimated, as a result of which the coefficients get a variance different from zero. As our aim is to include as many alternatives as possible in the forecast, we shall take the second course. However, there is one exception to the extent that only homoskedastic models without autocorrelation are taken into consideration. This reduces the number of unknown parameters considerably. Moreover – as it has been said before – the fact that only linear models are admitted further limits the number of alternatives. In short, the set of alternatives wil be restricted to models that can be described as follows:

$$\mathbf{w}_t = \Pi X_t + \mathbf{v}_t \tag{3.17}$$

in which $\mathbf{w}_t$ is a vector with length G, X_t a non-stochastic vector k, Π a matrix of unknown coefficients of the order $G \times k$ and $\mathbf{v}_t$ a vector of disturbances, independently distributed as $N(O, \Sigma)$ with unknown $G \times G$ matrix Σ, which is independent of t.

The set of models is now made up from variants on (3.17) with different exogeneous variables and therefore different Π_i, as well as different possible lengths of $\mathbf{w}_t$, provided $\mathbf{w}_t$ contains the vector $\mathbf{y}_t$.

3.3.2

LEMMA 1

The *optimal linear forecasting* procedure for model (3.17) according to (3.4) and (3.5) is for the year τ

$$\hat{\mathbf{w}}_\tau = \mathbf{P} X_\tau \tag{3.18}$$ [7]

in which $\mathbf{P}$ is the least squares estimate of Π.

So

$$\mathbf{P} = \mathbf{W}'X(X'X)^{-1} \tag{3.19}$$

in which X' and $\mathbf{W}'$ are the matrices respectively of the order $k \times T$ and $G \times T$ $(k<T)$.

Before proving this we shall first show in point A which forecasting procedure is the optimal one with a different notation of model (3.17) and afterwards we shall translate the result in the original notation in point B. We mainly follow Goldberger (1964, pp. 246 and 232).

A. According to (3.17) for the ith component of $\mathbf{w}_t$ the following holds

$$\mathbf{w}_{it} = \Pi_{i\cdot}x_t + \mathbf{v}_{it} = x_t'\Pi_{i\cdot}' + \mathbf{v}_{it} = x_t'\beta_i + \mathbf{v}_{it}$$

in which $\beta_i = \Pi_i'$ is the ith row of Π written as a column.

When the T observations of equation i are written under each other we get

$$\begin{bmatrix} \mathbf{w}_{i1} \\ \vdots \\ \mathbf{w}_{iT} \end{bmatrix} = \begin{bmatrix} X_{11} & \cdots & X_{1k} \\ & \vdots & \\ X_{T1} & \cdots & X_{Tk} \end{bmatrix} \begin{bmatrix} \beta_{i1} \\ \vdots \\ \beta_{ik} \end{bmatrix} + \begin{bmatrix} \mathbf{v}_{i1} \\ \vdots \\ \mathbf{v}_{iT} \end{bmatrix}$$

or, more compact

$$\mathbf{w}_i = X\beta_i + \mathbf{v}_i .$$

When all G equations are then written under each other we have

$$\mathbf{h} = Z\beta + \boldsymbol{\varepsilon} \tag{3.20}$$

in which

$$\mathbf{h} = \begin{bmatrix} \mathbf{w}_1 \\ \mathbf{w}_2 \\ \vdots \\ \mathbf{w}_G \end{bmatrix} \quad Z = \begin{bmatrix} X & & & \\ & X & & \\ & & \ddots & \\ & & & X \end{bmatrix} \quad \beta = \begin{bmatrix} \beta_1 \\ \beta_2 \\ \vdots \\ \beta_G \end{bmatrix} \quad \text{and} \quad \boldsymbol{\varepsilon} = \begin{bmatrix} \mathbf{v}_1 \\ \mathbf{v}_2 \\ \vdots \\ \mathbf{v}_G \end{bmatrix} \tag{3.21}$$

in this: $\mathbf{h}$ is a vector with length $G \times T$

β is a vector with length $G \times k$

$\boldsymbol{\varepsilon}$ is a vector with length $G \times T$

Z is a matrix of $(G \times T)$ to $(G \times k)$ with given values and rank $G \times k$.

For the disturbance $\boldsymbol{\varepsilon}$ it follows from the distribution of $\mathbf{v}_t$ that

$$E\boldsymbol{\varepsilon} = 0 \tag{3.22}$$

and

$$\mathscr{V}(\boldsymbol{\varepsilon}) \stackrel{\text{def}}{=} E\boldsymbol{\varepsilon}\boldsymbol{\varepsilon}' = \Sigma \otimes I_T = \Psi \tag{3.23}$$

in which $\otimes$ is the Kroneckermatrixproduct and I_T a unity matrix of the order T. (3.20) can now be interpreted as the generalized linear regression model. For this model the optimal procedure for the forecast in period τ is

$$\hat{\mathbf{h}}_\tau = Z_\tau \hat{\beta}$$

in which $\hat{\beta}$ is the generalized least squares estimator.

Proof

Assume

$$\hat{\mathbf{h}}_\tau = Z_\tau \tilde{\boldsymbol{\beta}}$$

in which

$$\tilde{\boldsymbol{\beta}} = [(Z'\Psi^{-1}Z)^{-1} Z'\Psi^{-1} + D']\,\mathbf{h} = C'\mathbf{h} \tag{3.24}$$

and D an arbitrary matrix of the order $(G \times k)$ to $(G \times k)$.

For $\mathbf{e}_\tau$ the vector with forecasting errors in the period τ it now holds that

$$\mathbf{e}_\tau = \hat{\mathbf{h}}_\tau - \mathbf{h}_\tau = Z_\tau(\tilde{\boldsymbol{\beta}} - \beta) - \boldsymbol{\varepsilon}_\tau . \tag{3.25}$$

If $\hat{\mathbf{h}}_\tau$ is to be the optimal forecast of $\mathbf{h}_\tau$ then, on account of (3.4) $E\mathbf{e}_\tau = 0$ must hold and, consequently, according to (3.25) and (3.22)

$$EZ_\tau\tilde{\boldsymbol{\beta}} = Z_\tau\beta \quad \text{or} \quad E\tilde{\boldsymbol{\beta}} = \beta$$

hence, on account of (3.24), (3.20) and (3.22)

$$\begin{aligned} Z_\tau\beta = Z_\tau E\tilde{\boldsymbol{\beta}} = Z_\tau C' E\mathbf{h} &= Z_\tau C' Z\beta \\ &= Z_\tau [I + D'Z]\,\beta \end{aligned}$$

and consequently

$$D'Z = 0 \quad \text{and} \quad \tilde{\boldsymbol{\beta}} = C'(Z\beta + \boldsymbol{\varepsilon}) = \beta + C'\boldsymbol{\varepsilon}$$

so that

$$\mathscr{V}(\tilde{\boldsymbol{\beta}}) = C'[E\boldsymbol{\varepsilon}\boldsymbol{\varepsilon}']\,C = C'\Psi C$$

or

$$\mathscr{V}(\tilde{\boldsymbol{\beta}}) = (Z'\Psi^{-1}Z)^{-1} + D'\Psi D \tag{3.26}$$

because of

$$D'Z = 0.$$

For the optimality of $\hat{\mathbf{h}}_\tau$ it is further required according to (3.5) that: $\det \mathscr{V}(\mathbf{e}_\tau)$ is a minimum. If τ refers to a future period then $\boldsymbol{\varepsilon}_\tau$ and $\boldsymbol{\varepsilon}$ and consequently also $\boldsymbol{\varepsilon}_\tau$ and $\mathbf{h}$ or $\boldsymbol{\varepsilon}_\tau$ and $\tilde{\boldsymbol{\beta}}$ are mutually independent, so that it follows from (3.25)

$$\mathscr{V}(\mathbf{e}_\tau) = Z_\tau \mathscr{V}(\tilde{\boldsymbol{\beta}}) Z'_\tau + \mathscr{V}(\boldsymbol{\varepsilon}_\tau). \tag{3.27}$$

If τ refers to a forecasting term of one period then $\boldsymbol{\varepsilon}_\tau = \mathbf{v}_\tau$ where $\mathbf{v}_\tau$ is given in (3.17) so that (3.27) with the help of (3.26) and (3.23) becomes

$$\begin{aligned} \mathscr{V}(\mathbf{e}_\tau) &= Z_\tau [(Z'\Psi^{-1}Z)^{-1} + D'\Psi D] Z'_\tau + \Sigma \\ &= Z_\tau (Z'\Psi^{-1}Z)^{-1} Z'_\tau + Z_\tau D'\Psi D Z'_\tau + \Sigma . \end{aligned}$$

As it is $Z'\Psi^{-1}Z$ and $D'\Psi D$ are positive definite respectively semidefinite so that[8]

$$\begin{aligned} \det \mathscr{V}(\mathbf{e}_\tau) &\geqslant \det Z_\tau (Z'\Psi^{-1}Z)^{-1} Z'_\tau + \det Z_\tau D'\Psi D Z'_\tau + \det \Sigma \\ &\geqslant \det Z_\tau (Z'\Psi^{-1}Z)^{-1} Z'_\tau + \det \Sigma \end{aligned}$$

So the optimal forecasting procedure is obtained for $D=0$ or, by way of (3.24)

$$\hat{\mathbf{h}}_\tau = Z_\tau [(Z'\Psi^{-1}Z)^{-1} Z'\Psi^{-1}] \mathbf{h} \tag{3.28}$$ [9]

with variance-covariance matrix of forecasting errors

$$\mathscr{V}(\mathbf{e}_\tau) = Z_\tau (Z'\Psi^{-1}Z)^{-1} Z'_\tau + \Sigma . \tag{3.29}$$

B. (3.28) and (3.18) must yet be proved to be identical. We apply the rules for the Kroneckermatrix multiplications.[10]

Z and Z_τ can be written as

$$\begin{aligned} Z &= I_G \otimes X \\ Z_\tau &= I_G \otimes X'_\tau . \end{aligned} \tag{3.30}$$

With the help of (3.23) we can write

$$\begin{aligned} (Z'\Psi^{-1}Z)^{-1} &= [(I_G \otimes X)' (\Sigma \otimes I_T)^{-1} (I_G \otimes X)]^{-1} \\ &= [(I_G \otimes X') (\Sigma^{-1} \otimes I_T) (I_G \otimes X)]^{-1} \\ &= [\Sigma^{-1} \otimes (X'X)]^{-1} \\ &= \Sigma \otimes (X'X)^{-1} . \end{aligned} \tag{3.31}$$

Substitution of (3.31), (3.30) and (3.23) in (3.28) gives

$$\begin{aligned}\hat{\mathbf{h}}_\tau &= [I_G \otimes X'_\tau]\,[\Sigma \otimes (X'X)^{-1}]\,[I_G \otimes X]'\,[\Sigma \otimes I_T]^{-1}\,\mathbf{h}\\ &= [I_G \otimes X'_\tau]\,[\Sigma \otimes (X'X)^{-1}]\,[I_G \otimes X']\,[\Sigma^{-1} \otimes I_T]\,\mathbf{h}\\ &= [I_G \otimes X'_\tau(X'X)^{-1}\,X']\,\mathbf{h}\,.\end{aligned}$$

So

$$\hat{\mathbf{h}}_\tau = \begin{bmatrix}\hat{\mathbf{w}}_{1\tau}\\ \hat{\mathbf{w}}_{2\tau}\\ \vdots\\ \hat{\mathbf{w}}_{G\tau}\end{bmatrix} = $$

$$= \begin{bmatrix} X'_\tau(X'X)^{-1}\,X' & & & \\ & X'_\tau(X'X)^{-1}\,X' & & \\ & & \ddots & \\ & & & X'_\tau(X'X)^{-1}\,X'\end{bmatrix}\begin{bmatrix}\mathbf{w}_1\\ \mathbf{w}_2\\ \vdots\\ \mathbf{w}_G\end{bmatrix}.$$

Taking into account that $X'_\tau(X'X)^{-1}\,X'\mathbf{w}_i$ is a scalar it further follows that

$$\hat{\mathbf{h}}_\tau = \begin{bmatrix}\hat{\mathbf{w}}_{1\tau}\\ \hat{\mathbf{w}}_{2\tau}\\ \vdots\\ \hat{\mathbf{w}}_{G}\end{bmatrix} = \begin{bmatrix}X'_\tau(X'X)^{-1}\,X\mathbf{w}_1\\ X'_\tau(X'X)^{-1}\,X\mathbf{w}_2\\ \vdots\\ X'_\tau(X'X)^{-1}\,X\mathbf{w}_G\end{bmatrix} =$$

$$= \begin{bmatrix}\mathbf{w}'_1X'\,(X'X)^{-1}\,X_\tau\\ \mathbf{w}'_2X'\,(X'X)^{-1}\,X_\tau\\ \vdots\\ \mathbf{w}'_GX'\,(X'X)^{-1}\,X_\tau\end{bmatrix} = \mathbf{W}X'\,(X'X)^{-1}\,X_\tau\,.$$

It is notable in all this that it is possible to derive the optimal forecasting procedure without giving one's opinion upon Σ. I.e. (3.18) is the optimal forecasting procedure corresponding to (3.17) regardless of the value of Σ, provided the latter is non singular. The above result proceeded from the fact that all equations contain the same exogeneous variables. Zellner (1962) has shown that the least squares estimation per equation is no longer optimal, when the matrix Π contains zero's. In that case the optimal estimator derived from our rules does indeed depend on Σ.

The fact that in our case **P** is independent of Σ, – to this extent that the estimation formula (3.19) contains neither Σ nor an estimation of Σ – has the following consequences: If only $\mathbf{y}_\tau$ is to be forecasted, i.e. a subvector of $\mathbf{w}_\tau$, the optimal forecasting procedure for $\mathbf{y}_\tau$ does not change when $\mathbf{w}_\tau$ is extended. This indicates implicitly that the extension mentioned is superfluous in that case. The *optimal number of equations* can be proved more formally analogous to the proof in Subsection 3.2.2.

We have:

Model G: The model incorporated in (3.17) with corresponding assumptions for $\mathbf{v}_t$.

Model m: The submodel that only contains $\mathbf{y}_t$.

On the basis of (3.29), (3.30) and (3.31) we can write

$$\begin{aligned}\mathscr{V}(\mathbf{e}_\tau) &= [I_G \otimes X_\tau'] [\Sigma \otimes (X'X)^{-1}] [I_G \otimes X_\tau']' + \Sigma \qquad (3.31a)\\ &= \Sigma \otimes X_\tau'(X'X)^{-1} X_\tau' + \Sigma \\ &= \Sigma \otimes \quad q_\tau \quad + \Sigma \\ &= \Sigma q_\tau + \Sigma \\ &= (q_\tau + 1)\, \Sigma \qquad (3.32)\end{aligned}$$

for

$$q_\tau = X_\tau'(X'X)^{-1} X_\tau \qquad (3.33)$$

is a (non-stochastic) scalar.

Since $\boldsymbol{\varepsilon}$ and consequently also $\mathbf{h}$, $\tilde{\boldsymbol{\beta}}$ and $\mathbf{e}_\tau$ are normally distributed $\mathbf{e}_\tau'[V(\mathbf{e}_\tau)]^{-1}\, \mathbf{e}_\tau$ has a χ^2-distribution with G degrees of freedom. So the forecasting interval of model G is

$$\mathbf{e}_\tau' [(1 + q_\tau)\, \Sigma]^{-1}\, e_\tau \leqslant \chi^2(G)$$

or

$$\mathbf{e}_\tau' \Sigma^{-1} \mathbf{e}_\tau \leqslant (1 + q_\tau)\, \chi^2(G). \qquad (3.34)$$

In the same way the following can be derived for model m

$$\mathbf{e}_{1\tau}' \Sigma_{11}^{-1} \mathbf{e}_{1\tau} \leqslant (1 + q_\tau)\, \chi^2(m) \qquad (3.35)$$

in which the indices 1 and 11 give the appropriate partitioning of $\mathbf{e}_t$ and Σ. Again, from (3.34) the projection in the m-dimensional space follows, namely

$$\mathbf{e}_{1\tau}' \Sigma_{11}^{-1} \mathbf{e}_{1\tau} \leqslant (1 + q_\tau)\, \chi^2(G).$$

This is again larger than the space indicated by (3.35) so one may state on the same grounds as before that extension of a model with more equations does not result in a smaller forecasting interval. We can formulate this in the following lemma.

LEMMA 2

If it is possible to describe all models of the set on the basis of which the forecast $\mathbf{y}_t$ can be made by

$$\mathbf{w}_t \cong N(\Pi X_t, \Psi)$$

with given values X_τ in the forecasting period $t=\tau$, an unknown matrix Π and known or unknown non-singular Ψ and if there are no restrictions for Π, then in a selection according to Summary 1 only those models need be considered for which $\mathbf{w}_t=\mathbf{y}_t$ and consequently $G=m$. So in that case the optimal forecasting procedure (3.18) will always contain m equations only.

3.3.3

Assume the following model is given

$$\mathbf{y}_t = \Pi X_t + \mathbf{v}_t \tag{3.36}$$

with

$$\mathbf{v}_t \cong N(0, \Sigma)$$

then the optimal forecasting procedure is according to (3.18)

$$\mathbf{y}_t = \mathbf{P} X_\tau$$

with

$$\mathbf{P} = \mathbf{Y}' X (X'X)^{-1} \tag{3.37}$$

and X_τ a columnvector with the k values of the exogeneous variables in the forecasting period. For the variance-covariance matrix of the forecasting errors we get according to (3.32)

$$\mathscr{V}(\mathbf{e}_\tau) = \Omega_\tau = (1 + q_\tau)\,\Sigma\,.$$

A comparison of (3.36) on the basis of Summary 1 with a model with as many equations but with partly different exogeneous variables requires the calculation of

$$\det c_\alpha \Omega = \det (1 + q_\tau)\, \chi^2_\alpha (m)\, \Sigma\,.$$

As Σ is usually no more known than Π, we replace Σ by the unbiased estimator S, defined as

$$S = \frac{YY' - PX'XP'}{T - k}. \tag{3.38}$$

We then get, dropping the index τ

$$\hat{\Omega} = (1 + q)\, S. \tag{3.39}$$

According to Hooper and Zellner (1961) the magnitude

$$\frac{T - k - m + 1}{(T - k)\, m}\, \mathbf{e}_t' \hat{\Omega}^{-1} \mathbf{e}_t$$

has an F-distribution with m and $T-k-m+1$ degrees of freedom.

So a choice of the models according to the smallest $(1-\alpha)\%$ confidence interval means selection according to the volume of the domain bounded by the ellipsoid

$$\frac{T - k - m + 1}{(T - k)\, m}\, \mathbf{e}_t' \hat{\Omega}^{-1} \mathbf{e}_t = F_\alpha(m, T - k - m + 1) \tag{3.40}$$

or selection according to $\det \theta \hat{\Omega}$ which comes to the same thing, with θ defined as

$$\theta = \frac{(T - k)\, m}{T - k - m + 1}\, F_\alpha(m, T - k - m + 1). \tag{3.41}$$

This implies a deviation from Summary 1 as a known Ω was assumed there.

Summary 2

From the set of models that model and corresponding procedure will be selected for which

$$\boxed{E\mathbf{e}_t = 0} \tag{3.4}$$

and

$$\boxed{\det \theta_\alpha \hat{\Omega} \quad \text{a minimum}} \tag{3.42}$$

provided $\hat{\Omega}$ is non-singular and $\mathbf{y}_t$ is the same vector with length m in all models.

The disadvantage of (3.42) as a standard for selection is that for different values of k it is dependent on α. For, according to (3.42) model i is preferable to model j if $\det\theta_i\hat{\Omega}_i < \det\theta_j\hat{\Omega}_j$ or by way of (3.41)

$$\frac{\det\hat{\Omega}_i}{\det\hat{\Omega}_j} < \left(\frac{\theta_j}{\theta_i}\right)^m = \left(\frac{F_{\alpha,\,T-k_j}}{F_{\alpha,\,T-k_i}}\right)^m \frac{(T-k_j)(T-k_i-m+1)}{(T-k_j-m+1)(T-k_i)}.$$

For $k_i \neq k_j$ the ratio $F_{\alpha,T-k_j}/F_{\alpha,T-k_i}$ depends on α, as one glance at an F-table shows. On the other hand, a standard that is independent of α, like $\det\Omega$, insufficiently stresses the fact that a model should be as simple

TABLE III.1[a]

Some values of θ_α with $\alpha = 0.05$

↓ T-k / m→	1	2	3	4	5	6	7	8	9	10
1	161.4	-	-	-	-	-	-	-	-	-
2	18.51	798	-	-	-	-	-	-	-	-
3	10.13	57.00	1941	-	-	-	-	-	-	-
4	7.71	25.47	115.0	3594	-	-	-	-	-	-
5	6.61	17.35	46.40	192.5	5755	-	-	-	-	-
6	5.99	13.90	29.66	72.96	289.5	8424	-	-	-	-
7	5.59	11.99	22.72	44.73	105.1	405.9	11603	-	-	-
8	5.32	10.83	19.04	33.22	62.60	143.0	543	15290	-	-
9	5.12	10.04	16.78	27.18	45.45	83.16	186.7	697	19480	-
10	4.96	9.47	15.26	23.54	36.58	59.40	106.6	236.0	872	24190
11	4.84	9.02	14.15	21.12	31.19	47.08	75.15	132.9	290.7	1066.5
12	4.75	8.68	13.36	19.36	27.68	39.81	58.94	92.54	162.0	351.2
13	4.67	8.41	12.73	18.10	25.13	34.91	49.27	71.93	103.3	193.7
14	4.60	8.18	12.22	17.11	23.31	31.45	42.88	59.68	86.10	132.7
15	4.54	8.01	11.80	16.30	21.82	28.98	38.38	51.60	70.97	101.5
16	4.49	7.85	11.45	15.66	20.73	26.97	35.17	45.94	61.02	82.97
17	4.45	7.71	11.19	15.11	19.75	25.50	32.56	41.75	54.06	70.98
18	4.41	7.60	10.94	14.69	19.03	24.26	30.66	38.62	48.92	62.60
19	4.38	7.49	10.73	14.30	18.37	23.21	29.06	36.10	45.08	56.43
20	4.35	7.41	10.53	13.93	17.81	22.32	27.70	34.09	42.00	52.00
30	4.17	6.89	9.48	12.13	14.94	17.93	21.26	24.83	28.84	33.14
60	4.00	6.41	8.59	10.66	12.74	14.86	16.99	19.18	21.41	23.81
∞	3.84	6.00	7.80	9.48	11.05	12.54	14.07	15.52	16.92	18.30

[a] Calculated by means of (3.41) and a standard F-table e.g. Pearson and Hartley (1966, p. 171).

as possible. For, when $k_j > k_i$ we usually have $\theta_j > \theta_i$[11] and so

$$\frac{\det \hat{\Omega}_i}{\det \hat{\Omega}_j} < \frac{\theta_i^m}{\theta_j^m} \frac{\det \hat{\Omega}_i}{\det \hat{\Omega}_j} = \frac{\det \theta_i \hat{\Omega}_i}{\det \theta_j \hat{\Omega}_j}.$$

Moreover, the calculation of $\theta_\alpha \hat{\Omega}$ immediately provides the possibility to give interval forecasts. Since the 95% forecasting intervals already give such wide margins for the most important variables, no wider forecasting intervals (99% or 99.9%) have been calculated, although θ_i/θ_j usually decreases with decreasing α. Here det $\theta_{0.05}\hat{\Omega}$ was chosen as a standard for selection so with $\alpha = 0.05$. The value of θ for different values of m and $T-k$ appears from Table III.1, all the time for $\alpha = 0.05$. From now on we shall leave out the indication α or 0.05 and we shall write the criterion as

$$\det \theta \hat{\Omega} \quad \text{a minimum}$$ [12].

3.3.4

If the forecasting period contains h years with $h > 1$, the accuracy of the prediction for each of the h years must be taken into account. We shall derive the simultaneous forecasting interval for this situation below.

We start with (3.30) now written as

$$\begin{aligned} Z &= I_m \otimes X \\ Z &= I_m \otimes X'_\tau \end{aligned} \tag{3.43}$$

in which the *vector* X'_τ in (3.30) has been replaced by a $(\tau \times k)$ *matrix* X'_τ in (3.43) with given values of the k exogeneous variables for each of the h years that are to be forecasted.[13] Analogous to (3.31a) we can now write

$$\mathscr{V}(\mathbf{e}_\tau) = [I_m \otimes X'_\tau] [\Sigma \otimes (X'X)^{-1}] [I_m \otimes X_\tau] + \Sigma \otimes I_\tau .$$

The unity matrix in the last term reflects the assumption that the disturbances of the various years are independent. By applying the rules of the Kroneckermatrix product we get

$$\begin{aligned} \mathscr{V}(\mathbf{e}_\tau) &= \Sigma \otimes X'_\tau (X'X)^{-1} X_\tau + \Sigma \otimes I_\tau \\ &= \Sigma \otimes [M + I_\tau] \end{aligned} \tag{3.44}$$

in which

$$M = X'_\tau (X'X)^{-1} X_\tau \tag{3.45}$$

For $h = 1$, M becomes q – see (3.33).

The $(1-\alpha)$ % forecasting interval becomes

$$\mathbf{e}'_\tau [\mathscr{V}(\mathbf{e}_\tau)]^{-1} \mathbf{e}_\tau \leqslant \chi^2(m)$$

in which $\chi^2(m)$ is independent of τ and $\mathscr{V}(\mathbf{e}_\tau)$ is given in (3.44). For an estimation of the interval Σ is replaced by S defined in (3.38) so that the interval becomes

$$\mathbf{e}'_\tau \hat{\Omega}_\tau^{-1} \mathbf{e}_\tau \leqslant \theta_\alpha$$

with θ_α independent of τ and

$$\hat{\Omega}_\tau = S \otimes [M + I_\tau]$$

for $m=1$ this becomes

$$\hat{\Omega}_\tau = s^2 [M + I_\tau]. \tag{3.46}$$

In Section 5.2 an example of the latter will be given.

3.3.5

Finally, one may wonder in what way the situation is changed if not all equations of the model contain the same exogeneous variables, so if the matrix Π contains zero's. This is the case discussed by Zellner (1962). Goldberger (1964, p. 262) puts the problem in the frame of the choosing of 0 coefficients in reduced forms. One may well imagine this situation. It is indeed possible that for some models the reduced form and the structural form coincide. The model can also be recursive, partly or totally, so that zero elements may occur in Π, e.g. when $\mathbf{y}_{it}$ is indeed dependent on the other components of $\mathbf{y}_t$, yet does not itself help to determine them, whereas X_{kt} is a specific explanatory variable of $\mathbf{y}_{it}$ only.

Zellner shows that if Π contains any zero's least squares per equation is no longer optimal. (3.18) or its counterpart with zerocoefficients is no more optimal then. This is apparent from the fact that in that case the Σ can not be eliminated as it happens in the working-out of (3.28). The optimal forecasting procedure becomes dependent on Σ. Lemma 2 can not be applied either. It is conceivable that additional equations put so many restrictions on the derived form that the projection of the G-dimensional forecasting space has a smaller volume in the required m-dimensions than the forecasting area that would have been obtained by neglecting the additional equations. This situation has not been investigated any further.

One should realise that the weighted square forecasting error usually no longer follows an F-distribution in the described case (see Anderson, 1958, p. 193 ff.). The problem of the distribution and the number of the degrees of freedom does not come up with Zellner, since he deals only with equations that contain an equal number of exogeneous variables.

3.4. Evaluated forecasts

3.4.1

The criterion for selection $\det \theta\hat{\Omega}$ or the contents V of the volume bounded by the ellipsoid $\mathbf{e}_t'(\theta\hat{\Omega})^{-1}\,\mathbf{e}_t = 1$ is based on the equal evaluation of the various elements of $\mathbf{e}_t$. As previously said, it is often difficult to disconnect the problem of the evaluation from the specific aim for which the forecast is made. When there are several variables to be predicted or one variable for more than one period, a weighing problem arises that does not exist in scalar-forecasts, namely how are the forecasting errors of different variables or of the different moments of one variable evaluated against each other. Also these evaluations depend in the end on the purpose for which the forecast is made, but one can investigate in what way the choice of the model is influenced in certain cases by a strong preference for a good forecast of $\mathbf{y}_{it}$.

As it is, the selection as described above is invariant against the choice of units. This implies that an evaluation of the forecasting errors that is a linear transformation of these forecasting errors, does not influence the choice either. This is clear when we select according to so-called *evaluated* forecasting errors $\boldsymbol{\delta}_t$, in which

$$\boldsymbol{\delta}_t = M\mathbf{e}_t\,. \tag{3.47}$$

In this M is a constant $m \times m$ matrix of weighing coefficients.

Since

$$\det E\boldsymbol{\delta}_t\boldsymbol{\delta}_t' = \det ME\mathbf{e}_t\mathbf{e}_t'M = (\det M)^2 \det \hat{\Omega}$$

the selection is not influenced. Not everybody will indeed use the same M. So the evaluation of the forecast will differ per individual. However, as long as everybody sticks to his own M with rank m for the different models, the same model will be optimal for everyone when our standard is used.

The situation changes when the roworder of M is lower than m. A special case occurs when M is a vector $\vec{M}$. Then $\mathbf{e}_t$ is reduced to a scalar $\boldsymbol{\delta}_t$. In general, when the consequences of the forecasting errors can be translated into one single indicator, *the loss-function* $\mathbf{Z}_t = Z(\mathbf{e}_1, \mathbf{e}_2, \ldots, \mathbf{e}_m)$, one will base oneself in the selection on the mathematical expectation of the loss, so on $E\mathbf{z}_t$ or on an estimation of it. This is only to the point if $\mathbf{Z}_t$ is a non-linear function of $\mathbf{e}_i$ or if $E\mathbf{e}_i \neq 0$ for at least *one i*. Otherwise $E\mathbf{z}$ is always 0. For a quadratic loss-function $\mathbf{Z} = \mathbf{e}_t' W \mathbf{e}_t$ a selection according to the mathematical expectation gives

$$E\mathbf{z} = E \text{ trace } \mathbf{e}_t' W \mathbf{e}_t = \text{trace } W E \mathbf{e}_t \mathbf{e}_t' = \text{trace } W\Omega \qquad (3.47a)$$

and trace $W\hat{\Omega}$ as the estimator of this.

3.4.2

We have made use of another possibility by selecting according to the damage connected with a certain forecasting interval. If we indicate this damage by $\mathscr{D}$ we find that

$$\mathscr{D} = \int \cdots \int_{\mathbf{e}'_t \hat{\Omega}^{-1} \mathbf{e}_t \leqslant \theta} Z(\mathbf{e}_1, \mathbf{e}_2, \ldots, \mathbf{e}_m) \, d\mathbf{e}_1 \ldots d\mathbf{e}_m . \qquad (3.48)$$

We start by choosing a quadratic loss-function

$$Z = \mathbf{e}_t' W \mathbf{e}_t \qquad (3.49)$$

in which W is the $m \times m$ matrix of the weighingcoefficients which represent the damage that is caused by the various combinations of the forecasting errors.

For $m=2$ the relationship has been sketched in Figure III.1.

A kind of 'chalice' is formed that is cut by a cylinder. The content of that part of the cylinder that is outside the 'chalice' and above the base – the ellips $\mathbf{e}_t' \, \hat{\Omega}^{-1} \mathbf{e}_t \leqslant \theta$ – represents the total damage, connected with the forecast of a certain model.

Leaving the evaluations out of account M_i would have been chosen rather than M_j if for positive $\det \hat{\Omega}_k$

$$\det \theta_i \hat{\Omega}_i < \det \theta_j \hat{\Omega}_j$$

or in other words if the content of the space

$$\mathbf{e}_t' \Omega_i^{-1} \mathbf{e}_t \leqslant \theta_i \qquad (3.50)$$

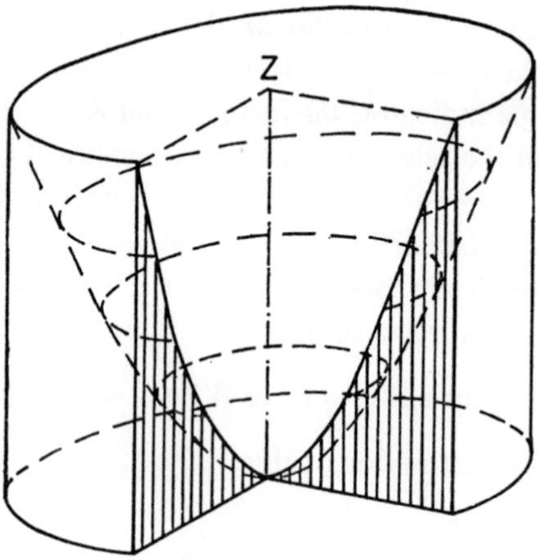

Fig. III.1.

is smaller than the one of

$$\mathbf{e}_t'\hat{\Omega}_j^{-1}\mathbf{e}_t \leqslant \theta_j. \tag{3.51}$$

The evaluation of (3.50) according to (3.49) is, when leaving out the modelindicator i,

$$\mathscr{D} = \int_{\mathbf{e}'_t\hat{\Omega}^{-1}\mathbf{e}_t \leqslant \theta} \cdots \int \mathbf{e}_t' W \mathbf{e}_t \, \mathrm{d}e_{1t} \, \mathrm{d}e_{2t} \ldots \mathrm{d}e_{mt}. \tag{3.52}$$

For $m=2$ (see Figure 3.1) this is the content of the spatial figure described with the ellips for its base.

In order to modify (3.52) into a useful indicator a transformation is applied twice. First the form under the integrals is diagonalised. This takes place by way of the transformation

$$\delta_t = P^{-1}\mathbf{e}_t. \tag{3.53}$$

Substituted in (3.52) this gives

$$|\det P| \int_{\delta'_t P'\hat{\Omega}^{-1}P\delta_t \leqslant \theta} \cdots \int \delta_t' P' W P \delta_t \, \mathrm{d}\delta_{1t} \ldots \mathrm{d}\delta_{mt}. \tag{3.54}$$

Now, for a positive definite W[14]

$$PWP' = \Lambda \tag{3.55}$$

in which

$$\lambda_{ij} = 0 \quad \text{for} \quad i \neq j$$

$$\lambda_{ij} > 0 \quad \text{for} \quad i = j \quad \text{(the eigenvalues of } W)$$

and[15] $\det P = \pm 1$.

Choose $\det P = 1$.

Substitution of these results in (3.54) then gives

$$\mathscr{D} = \underset{\delta'_t D \delta_t \leqslant \theta}{\int \cdots \int} \delta'_t \Lambda \delta_t \, \mathrm{d}\delta_{1t} \ldots \mathrm{d}\delta_{mt} \tag{3.56}$$

in which

$$D = P' \hat{\Omega}^{-1} P. \tag{3.57}$$

For the second simplification we look for a transformation

$$\mathbf{v}_t = A^{-1} \boldsymbol{\delta}_t \tag{3.58}$$

such that[16]

$$\frac{1}{\theta} A' D A = I \tag{3.59}$$

and

$$A' \Lambda A = B \tag{3.60}$$

with $b_{jk} = 0$ for $k \neq j$.

The desired matrix A consists of the eigenvectors of $\Lambda - (1/\theta)\, D$, whereas the diagonal matrix B contains the corresponding eigenvalues.[17] (3.56) then becomes

$$\mathscr{D} = \det A \underset{\mathbf{v}'_t \mathbf{v}_t \leqslant 1}{\int \cdots \int} \mathrm{v}'_t B \mathrm{v}_t \, \mathrm{d}\mathrm{v}_{it} \ldots \mathrm{d}\mathrm{v}_{mt}. \tag{3.61}$$

Now define

$$C_k = \underset{\mathbf{v}'_t \mathbf{v}_t \leqslant 1}{\int \cdots \int} \mathrm{v}_{kt}^2 \, \mathrm{d}\mathrm{v}_{it} \cdots \mathrm{d}\mathrm{v}_{mt}.$$

As B is diagonal

$$\mathscr{D} = \det A\,[b_{11}C_1 + b_{22}C_2 + \cdots + b_{mm}C_m]. \tag{3.62}$$

According to Cramer (1946, p. 121)

$$C_k = \frac{\pi^{m/2}}{2\Gamma(m/2+2)}.$$

Substituted in (3.62) this gives

$$\mathscr{D} = \frac{\pi^{m/2} \det A \operatorname{trace} B}{2\Gamma(m/2+2)}. \tag{3.63}$$

This expression can be simplified even further. For, according to (3.59)

$$(\det A)^2 \det D/\theta = 1$$

and consequently

$$\det A = \frac{1}{\sqrt{\det D/\theta}} = \frac{\theta^{m/2}}{\sqrt{\det D}} = \frac{\theta^{m/2}}{\sqrt{\det \hat{\Omega}^{-1}}}$$

according to (3.59) and (3.57).

It further holds that

$$\Gamma\left(\frac{m}{2}+2\right) = \left(\frac{m}{2}+1\right)\Gamma\left(\frac{m}{2}+1\right)$$

If we substitute these results in (3.63) we get

$$\mathscr{D} = \frac{(\theta\pi)^{m/2} \operatorname{trace} B}{(m+2)\,\Gamma\left(\frac{m}{2}+1\right)\sqrt{\det \hat{\Omega}^{-1}}}$$

or

$$\mathscr{D} = \frac{\hat{V} \operatorname{trace} B}{m+2} \tag{3.64}$$

in which $\hat{V}$ is the estimated content of the unweighted space (3.7). According to Sections 3.2 and 3.3 model i is preferred to model j if

$$\hat{V}_i < \hat{V}_j.$$

In a quadratic weighing according to (3.49) model i is preferable if

$$\mathcal{D}_i < \mathcal{D}_j$$

or, according to (3.64),

$$\hat{V}_i \text{ trace } B_i < \hat{V}_j \text{ trace } B_j . \tag{3.65}$$

In order to see what is meant by B_i this matrix is transformed. Substitution of (3.60) and (3.55) and the proposition that trace ABC = *trace* BCA [18] lead to

$$\text{trace } B_i = \text{trace } WA_iA_i' \tag{3.66}$$

since

$$PP' = I . \tag{3.67}$$

From (3.57) and (3.59) follows $A_iA_i' = \theta_i P^{-1}\hat{\Omega}_i P^{-T}$.

Substitution in (3.66) then gives

$$\begin{aligned}\text{trace } B_i &= \theta_i \text{ trace } WP^{-1}\hat{\Omega}_i P^{-T}\\ &= \theta_i \text{ trace } W\hat{\Omega}_i .\end{aligned}$$

When on account of the unweighed forecasting errors M_i is preferred to M_j this preference may turn in case of a quadratic evaluation of the forecasting errors if one of the variables is very important in its consequences or if one of the variances is exceptionally large. Since in a selection according to the reduced forms and a confidence interval of 95% the m is the same in all models, it can be stated that in case of a quadratic evaluation of the forecasting errors M_i is preferred to M_j if

$$\sqrt{\det \theta_i\hat{\Omega}_i} \text{ trace } W\theta_i\hat{\Omega}_i < \sqrt{\det \theta_j\hat{\Omega}_j} \text{ trace } W\theta_j\hat{\Omega}_j .$$

The standard for selection is then

$$\boxed{\text{trace } W\theta\hat{\Omega}\sqrt{\det \theta\hat{\Omega}} .} \tag{3.68}$$

For a diagonal W or $\hat{\Omega}$ this becomes

$$\sqrt{\det \theta\hat{\Omega}} \text{ trace } W\theta\hat{\Omega} = \sqrt{\det \theta\hat{\Omega}}\,[w_1\sigma_1^2 + w_2\sigma_2^2 + \cdots + w_m\sigma_m^2] \tag{3.69}$$

in which σ_i^2 is the variance of the forecasting error $\mathbf{e}_{it}$.

If $\frac{\text{trace } W\theta_i\hat{\Omega}_i}{\text{trace } W\theta_j\hat{\Omega}_j} = 1$ selection according to (3.68) comes to the same as selection according to (3.42). So this is the case if

$$\text{trace } W(\theta_i\hat{\Omega}_i - \theta_j\hat{\Omega}_j) = 0, \quad \text{or if}$$

$$\text{trace } W(\theta_i\hat{\Lambda}_i - \theta_j\hat{\Lambda}_j) = 0, \quad \text{in which } \hat{\Lambda}_i \text{ contains the eigen-values of } \hat{\Omega}_i.$$

In other words, if

$$\theta_i \sum_r w_r\lambda_{ir} - \theta_j \sum_r w_r\lambda_{jr} = 0$$

so, if the *weighted* sum of the estimated eigenvalues of the variance-covariancematrix Ω is equal in both models. There are various matrices W that satisfy this.

If $\sqrt{\det\theta_i\hat{\Omega}_i} = \sqrt{\det\theta_j\hat{\Omega}_j}$ and $k_i = k_j$ (3.68) coincides with the estimate of (3.47a). This happens if

$$\sqrt{\prod_i \hat{\lambda}_i} = \sqrt{\prod_j \hat{\lambda}_j}$$

so if the *unweighted product* of the eigenvalues is equal in both models.

3.4.3

Another interesting relationship[19] occurs if the preference function is

$$Z = \sum_{j=1}^{m} |\mathbf{e}_{jt}| P_j. \tag{3.70}$$

Leaving out the underlining we get

$$\mathcal{G} = \int_{e'_t\hat{\Omega}^{-1}e_t \leqslant \theta} \cdots \int \sum_{j=1}^{m} |e_{jt}| P_j \, de_1 \ldots de_m. \tag{3.71}$$

We can now write

$$\frac{1}{\theta}\hat{\Omega}^{-1} = (TT')^{-1} = (T^{-1})' T^{-1}. \tag{3.72}$$

So

$$\mathcal{G} = \sum_{j=1}^{m} P_j \int_{(T^{-1}e_t)'(T^{-1}e_t) \leqslant 1} \cdots \int |e_{jt}| \, de_1 \ldots de_m. \tag{3.73}$$

Define $\overline{de} = de_1 \ldots de_m$ and further

$$T^{-1} e_t = y \quad \text{then} \quad \overline{de} = T\, \overline{dy}$$

so that

$$\mathscr{G} = \det T \sum_{j=1}^{m} P_i \int \cdots \int_{y'y<1} |T_{j\cdot} y| \, \overline{dy} . \tag{3.74}$$

Since $e_t = Ty$ and consequently $e_{jt} = T_{j\cdot} y$ in which $T_{j\cdot}$ is the jth row of T,

$$|e_{jt}| = |T_{j\cdot} y| .$$

Continuing the analysis we get

$$\mathscr{G} = \det T \sum_{j=1}^{m} P_j |T_{j\cdot}| \int \cdots \int_{y'y \leqslant 1} \left| \frac{T_{j\cdot} y}{|T_{j\cdot}|} \right| \overline{dy}$$

$$= \det T \sum_{j=1}^{m} P_j |T_{j\cdot}| \, C$$

in which C is the area of a sphere that is dependent neither on w_j nor on T.

For

$$|T_{j\cdot}| = \sqrt{t_{j1}^2 + t_{j2}^2 + \cdots + t_{jm}^2} \tag{3.75}$$

and consequently

$$\frac{T_{j\cdot}}{|T_{j\cdot}|} \quad \text{is a unity factor} .$$

So the magnitude C can be regarded as a constant that drops out in a comparison between models. The comparison takes place according to

$$\det T \sum_{j=1}^{m} P_j |T_{j\cdot}| . \tag{3.76}$$

Now, according to (3.72) $\det T = \sqrt{\det \theta \Omega}$.

(3.76) can also be written as

$$\boxed{\sqrt{\det \theta \Omega} \sum_{j=1}^{m} \sqrt{t_{ji}^2 w_j^2 + t_{j2}^2 w_j^2 + \cdots + t_{jm}^2 w_j^2}} \tag{3.77}$$

with the help of (3.75) and the relation

$$P_j = \sqrt{w_j^2}\,.$$

This (3.77) is the counterpart of (3.68).

For diagonal $\hat{\Omega}$ the following holds

$$\begin{aligned} t_{jk} &= 0 \quad \text{for} \quad j \neq k \\ &= \sigma_j^2 \qquad j = k\,. \end{aligned}$$

In that case (3.77) becomes

$$\sqrt{\det \theta \hat{\Omega}} \sum_{j=1}^{m} t_{jj} w_j$$

or

$$\sqrt{\det \theta \hat{\Omega}}\,[w_1\sigma_1 + w_2\sigma_2 + \cdots + w_m\sigma_m]\,. \tag{3.78}$$

This is the counterpart of (3.69).

NOTES TO CHAPTER III

[1] Van Winkel (1970, p. 89).

[2] E.g. with the estimation of the parameters in non-linear models such as e.g. Cobb-Douglas production functions. See Bradu and Mundlak (1970).

[3] See e.g. Theil (1971, p. 125 and 126).

[4] The complications that predictions more than one period in advance carry with them if the model contains lagged endogeneous variables are briefly indicated in Section 4.5.

[5] (3.15) must be distinguished from the conditional interval

$$\mathbf{e}'_t\,[\Psi^{-1}]_m\,\mathbf{e}_t \leqslant \chi_\alpha^2(G) \tag{N1}$$

in which $[\Psi^{-1}]_m$ is the mxm minor of Ψ^{-1} with the relevant (co)variances. (N1) only coincides with (3.15) if $\boldsymbol{\varepsilon}_t^0 = \boldsymbol{\eta}_t^0$ so with independent irrelevant variables.

[6] If only the ith variable must be predicted, we have

$$\begin{aligned} &\mathbf{e}_{it}^2 \leqslant \chi_\alpha^2(G)\sigma_i^2 \quad \text{or} \\ &|e_{it}| \leqslant \sqrt{\chi_\alpha^2(G)\,\sigma_i^2} \end{aligned} \tag{3.15a}$$

These are the boundaries proposed by Hymans (1968) as a basis for the publication of the interval of $\mathbf{e}_{it}$ when the model contains G variables. So in a way (3.15) is a generalisation of Hyman's formula. E.g. if the analyst wishes to consider the joint interval of $\mathbf{e}_{it}$ and $\mathbf{e}_{jt}$, the ellips

$$[\mathbf{e}_{it} \quad \mathbf{e}_{jt}] \begin{bmatrix} \Omega_{ii} & \Omega_{ij} \\ \Omega_{ji} & \Omega_{jj} \end{bmatrix}^{-1} \begin{bmatrix} \mathbf{e}_{it} \\ \mathbf{e}_{jt} \end{bmatrix} \leqslant \chi_\alpha^2(G) \tag{3.15b}$$

can be drawn, based on (3.15). In some cases the diagram of (3.15) will be a useful addition to (3.15a).

7 It is only shown that (3.18) is superior to all other *linear* forecasting procedures. As we restrict ourselves throughout to linear procedures only the indication 'linear' will be omitted in the pages hereafter. Moreover, according to Koerts and Abrahamse (1969, p. 16 ff.) if $m=1$, P is also the BUE of Π, when – as it is here – the distribution of the disturbances is normal. It follows from this that, if $m=1$, and $\mathbf{v}_t \cong N(0, \sigma^2)$ also forecasting procedures $\mathbf{P}^* X_t$ with $\mathbf{P}^*$ an arbitrary non-linear estimation of P result in a larger variance of the forecasting error than (3.18). For, according to Koerts and Abrahamse

$$\{\mathscr{V}(\mathbf{P}^*)^{-1} - \mathscr{V}(P)^{-1}\}$$

is a positive semidefinite matrix, so

$$X'_\tau \mathscr{V}(P^*)^{-1} X_\tau + \sigma^2 \geqslant X'_\tau \mathscr{V}(\mathbf{P})^{-1} X_\tau + \sigma^2$$

or according to (3.30) and (3.27)

$$\operatorname{Var} \mathbf{e}^*_\tau \geqslant \operatorname{Var} \mathbf{e}_\tau .$$

8 $\det(B+\Delta) \geqslant \det B + \det \Delta \geqslant \det B$ for symmetrical and positive definite respectively positive semi-definite B and Δ. See Mirsky (1955, p. 419) or Theorem 1.44 by Graybill (1961, p. 6).

9 $\mathbf{h}_\tau$ is a columnvector with length G.

10 See e.g. Neudecker (1968)

11 For $\alpha=0.05$ this is apparent from Table III.1.

12 If in spite of Lemma 2 the selection is also extended to models with $G>m$ endogeneous variables and, in doing so, one uses $\det \theta\hat{\Omega}$ or the forecasting interval $\mathbf{e}'_t \hat{\Omega}^{-1} \mathbf{e}_t \leqslant \leqslant \theta(G)$, then these models G are never selected because also $\theta(G) > \theta(m)$, at least for $\alpha=0.05$. This is apparent from Table III. 1. For other values of α it must yet be shown. An analytical proof is most complicated here.

13 The h as well as the m must have been fixed in advance by the setting of the problem.

14 Graybill (1961, p. 5).

15 Graybill (1961, p. 6).

16 The bold-facing in these derivations is not complete. $\hat{\Omega}$ is in fact a stochastic variable just as D, A, B and $\mathscr{D}$. However, W and the scalar C_k mentioned hereafter are not.

17 Mirsky (1955, p. 410).

18 Graybill (1961, p. 7).

19 The author thanks Dr. G. Laman of the University of Amsterdam for his help with the derivations of this section.

CHAPTER IV

THE SET OF ADMITTED MODELS AND THE WAY IN WHICH THE SELECTION IS CARRIED OUT

4.1. Introduction

The problem of the selection of a forecasting model has presented itself in practice since long. As we have argued in the previous sections, the principles that are used in the selection are not at all uniform and often obscure. Many questions which are all in fact aspects of the same general selection problem are often answered differently. It is interesting to notice that some of the indicators used are in fact specific forms of the standard proposed here. This will be demonstrated in this chapter in Section 4.2. For this purpose first the criterion for selection is broken up in its component parts. The earlier restrictions remain valid especially the fact that the set is only composed of reduced forms of linear stochastic models with unknown coefficients and normally distributed disturbances with expectation 0 and an unknown but constant variance-covariance matrix. Section 4.3 deals with the meaning of these restrictions and with the question whether testing is necessary and, if so, which testing. In Section 4.4 the question arises to what extent efficiency in the selection can be achieved. As it is, one need not always construct the whole set of admitted models before selecting the optimal procedure. Sometimes it is already apparent during the testing that a model can indeed be admitted but does not have a chance of being chosen in the selection. One would better drop such a model at once. We shall call such a model non-relevant then. So, in fact, the selection takes place on the basis of the set of relevant admitted models. Finally, in the last section of this chapter a few problems are broached, connected with the use of lagged process variables.

4.2. The composition of the criterion for selection and the standards used in practice

4.2.1. *The Composition of the Criterion*

In this section the criterion for selection that was presented in Chapter

III will be unraveled. We present the analysis in terms of an unweighted criterion, so on

$$\det \theta_{0.05} \hat{\Omega} \tag{4.1}$$

Since we shall restrict ourselves to a value of $\alpha = 0.05$ the subscript 0.05 attached to the value of θ in (4.1) can be neglected.

A first decomposition of (4.1) can be given by way of the analysis in Section 3.3. For according to (3.39)

$$\hat{\Omega} = (1 + q) S \tag{4.2}$$

in which S and q can be defined according to (3.38) respectively (3.33). When we substitute (4.2) in (4.1) we get

$$\det \theta \hat{\Omega} = \theta^m (1 + q)^m \det S \tag{4.3}$$

Now assume that the model and the forecasting procedure do not have any exogeneous variables apart from the constant. (4.3) then becomes

$$\det \theta \hat{\Omega} = \theta^m \left(1 + \frac{1}{T}\right)^m \det S \tag{4.4}$$

in which T is the size of the sample. For, in that case we have $X_\tau = 1$ and $X'X = T$, so that (3.33) becomes $q_\tau = 1/T$.

For (3.37) we then get a vector with length m and typical element

$$p_j = \frac{1}{T} \sum_{t=1}^{T} Y_{jt} = \bar{Y}_j \tag{4.5}$$

When we form the $m \times T$ matrix

$$y = \begin{bmatrix} y_{11} & \cdots & y_{1T} \\ \vdots & & \vdots \\ y_{m1} & \cdots & y_{mT} \end{bmatrix} \tag{4.6}$$

in which

$$y_{jt} = Y_{jt} - \bar{Y}_j$$

and when we define the $m \times T$ matrix

$$E' = Y - PX' \tag{4.7}$$

then it follows with the help of (3.38) for $k = 1$

$$(T - 1) S = E'E = YY' - PX'XP' = yy'$$

so that (4.4) can further be simplified to

$$\det \theta\hat{\Omega} = \frac{\theta^m \left(1 + \frac{1}{T}\right)^m \det yy'}{(T-1)^m} \tag{4.8}$$

If model and forecasting procedure contain, apart from the constant, a number of exogeneous variables and if we express these in deviations from their means over the reference period, we then may form the matrix

$$x = \begin{bmatrix} x_{11} & x_{12} & \cdots & x_{1(k-1)} \\ x_{21} & x_{22} & \cdots & x_{2(k-1)} \\ \vdots & \vdots & & \vdots \\ x_{T1} & x_{T2} & \cdots & x_{T(k-1)} \end{bmatrix} \tag{4.9}$$

in which

$$x_{ti} = X_{ti} - \frac{1}{T} \sum_{t=1}^{T} X_{ti}$$

We know that

$$X'X = \begin{bmatrix} T & \partial \\ 0 & x'x \end{bmatrix}$$

Hence, according to (3.33)

$$q = q_\tau = \frac{1}{T} + x_\tau'(x'x)^{-1} x_\tau \tag{4.10}$$ [1]

in which x_τ' is the rowvector with the k values of the exogeneous variables in the year τ expressed in deviations from their means over the reference period.

If we then partition $P = [p_0 \ p]$ in which p_0 is the column with the elements according to (4.5) then

$$\begin{aligned} (T-k)\,S = E'E &= YY' - PX'XP' \\ &= YY' - Tp_0p_0' - px'xp' \\ &= yy' - px'xp' \end{aligned} \tag{4.11}$$

So with the help of (4.3), (4.10) and (4.11) the standard for selection

$\det \theta \hat{\Omega}$ can be written as

$$\theta^m \left[\frac{1 + \frac{1}{T} + x'_\tau (x'x)^{-1}\, x_\tau}{T - k} \right]^m \det [yy' - px'xp'] \tag{4.12}$$

or

$$\theta^m \left[\frac{1 + \frac{1}{T} + x'_\tau (x'x)^{-1}\, x_\tau}{T - k} \right]^m \det yy' \det [I - (yy')^{-1}\, px'xp'] \tag{4.13}$$

When we define the $m \times m$ matrix

$$\mathscr{R} = (yy')^{-1}\, px'xp' \tag{4.14}$$

as the multidimensional analogon of the square of the multiple correlation coefficient, it follows that

$$\theta^m \left[\frac{1 + \frac{1}{T} + x'_\tau (x'x)^{-1}\, x_\tau}{T - k} \right]^m \det [I - \mathscr{R}] \tag{4.15}$$

is the standard for selection, since $\det yy'$ can be regarded as a constant in the selection and consequently can be eliminated from (4.13). When we start from a weighted criterion for selection, so from (3.68), then as is apparent from (3.39), (4.11), (4.14) and (4.15) this results in

$$\theta^m \left[\frac{1 + \frac{1}{T} + x'_\tau (x'x)^{-1}\, x_\tau}{T - k} \right]^m \sqrt{\det [I - \mathscr{R}]}\ \operatorname{trace} W yy' [I - \mathscr{R}]. \tag{4.16}$$

The various characteristics of the optimal forecasting model are now clear, namely:

(1) The *number of endogeneous variables* is restricted to the m magnitudes that must be forecasted.

(2) The adjustment to the observations is as good as possible (the matrix $\mathscr{R}$ as close as possible to the unity matrix).

(3) The adjustment of the various equations is as much as possible *in proportion to the damage* caused by the forecasting errors (minimal value of trace $Wyy'[I-\mathscr{R}]$.

(4) The *number of exogeneous variables* is as small as possible (low value of θ and k).

(5) The *value of the exogeneous variables* comes as close as possible to the mean over the reference period (x_τ close to 0).

4.2.2. *The Standards Used in Practice*

By way of the various characteristics the optimal model must possess it can now be investigated to what extent the various aspects are taken into account in practice.

We shall first bring up for discussion the number of equations of the model. Strangely enough this aspect is seldom paid any attention to in the literature. Only Cramer's analysis (1969, p. 112 ff.) has come to my knowledge. However, he deals with another problem, namely in what way a structural form should be built up in an investigation. Here we found that if one only wishes to make forecasts and if one limits oneself to reduced forms without restrictions, Lemma 2 can be applied. The number of equations is then equal to the number of variables that are to be forecasted. It is a pity that most constructors of forecasting models do not clearly indicate *what* in fact they wish to predict. However, it has been apparent in the previous paragraphs that the problem of the optimal model cannot be solved if both the variables that are to be forecasted and the desired forecasting period have not first been carefully indicated.

Assume that one wishes to predict only 1 variable. Then, according to Lemma 2, the optimal model consists of 1 equation and the standard for selection (4.15) is reduced to [2]

$$F_{0.05}(1, T-k)\left[1 + \frac{1}{T} + x_\tau'(x'x)^{-1}\,x_\tau\right]\frac{1-R^2}{T-k} \qquad (4.17)$$

in which R is the multiple correlationcoefficient. Should one choose the model – as it is sometimes done – of which R^2 comes closest to the value *one* then, compared to our standards, a number of aspects is neglected [3].

In the first place the number of exogeneous variables used for the forecast is then not taken into account. So a better standard is the correlation coefficient corrected for degrees of freedom[4] namely

$$\bar{R}^2 = \frac{T-1}{T-k}(1-R^2). \tag{4.18}$$

However, with (4.18) one does not quite meet the effect of the number of degrees of freedom used, because also the value of θ, or in this case $F_{0.05}(1, T-k)$ depends on $T-k$. As we have seen in Section 3.3 in Table III.1 $\theta_{0.05}$ is always smaller as $(T-k)$ is larger.

Apart from the degree of adjustment of the model to the observations in the past and the number of explanatory factors used to achieve that result, the degree of independence of the explanatory factors is also important. For this reason $\det x'x$ or $\det X'X$ indicated by COL[5] is sometimes added as an indicator to the results of the calculations. However, in doing so it is not indicated what part is played by this COL in the decision, especially not how low a value of $\det x'x$ should be in order to eliminate the R^2 or $\bar{R}^2$ as an indicator. In Equation (4.15) this factor shows up as part of the value q.

The next factor that plays a part in the selection deals with the values of the exogeneous variables in the future. More precisely put, the extent to which the values of the exogeneous variables for the period τ deviate from their means in the reference period. This is expressed in (4.15) in the vector x_τ. The combination of the 2 factors last-mentioned leads to the value of

$$q = x_\tau'(x'x)^{-1}\, x_\tau$$ [6]

If more than *one* variable must be forecasted the simplified formula (4.17) does not hold, but the selection takes place according to (4.15) or (4.16). So according to

$$\theta^m \left[\frac{1+\dfrac{1}{T}+x_\tau'(x'x)^{-1}\,x_\tau}{T-k}\right]^m \det\,[I-\mathscr{R}]$$

or

$$\left[\theta\,\frac{1+\dfrac{1}{T}+x_\tau'(x'x)^{-1}\,x_\tau}{T-k}\right]^{(m/2)+1} \sqrt{\det\,[I-\mathscr{R}]}\;\text{trace}\;Wyy'\,[I-\mathscr{R}]$$

Compared with the case $m=1$ two new aspects come to the front, namely the covariances between the forecasting errors of the endogeneous variables and the relative importance of a good forecast of the various magnitudes. In practice one is seldom interested in covariances. One acts as if $I-\mathscr{R}$ were diagonal. However, even if one would not consider the covariance important at all – i.e. W diagonal – these covariances are still important at least according to our weighing procedure by way of the term $\det[I-\mathscr{R}]^7$. The neglect of these covariances is stimulated by the concentration on separate equations which is usual in the construction of economic models. One tries to improve the forecasting performance per equation without paying attention to the interrelationship. In our line of thought this need not lead to optimal results. We prove this in the following way:

Suppose $\hat{\Omega}_A$ is the variance-covariancematrix of the forecasting errors of model A. Now assume that a number of exogeneous variables is replaced by others in such a way that *all diagonal elements* of the variance-covariance matrix are reduced without changing the value of θ. Call the newly acquired model B and the relevant variance-covariance matrix $\hat{\Omega}_B$.

So for the diagonal elements $(\hat{\omega}_B)_{ii}$ the following holds

$$(\hat{\omega}_B)_{ii} < (\hat{\omega}_A)_{ii} \qquad i = 1, 2, \ldots, m\,.$$

This relation does *not* imply $\det\hat{\Omega}_B < \det\hat{\Omega}_A$ and so it can not yet be said which model will be chosen. This is apparent from the following examples:

Example 1

$$\hat{\Omega}_A = \begin{bmatrix} 4 & 3 \\ 3 & 4 \end{bmatrix} \quad \text{and} \quad \hat{\Omega}_B = \begin{bmatrix} 3 & 1 \\ 1 & 3 \end{bmatrix}$$

Example 2

$$\hat{\Omega}_A = \begin{bmatrix} 5 & 4 \\ 4 & 4 \end{bmatrix} \quad \text{and} \quad \hat{\Omega}_B = \begin{bmatrix} 4\frac{1}{3} & 2 \\ 2 & 3 \end{bmatrix}.$$

In both examples $\det\hat{\Omega}_B > \det\hat{\Omega}_A$ holds, so that model B is not chosen in spite of the smaller variances per equation. If the relative evaluation of the forecasting errors is put in – in other words if there is a selection according to (3.68) – then in Example 1 model B proves to be in favour if W is diagonal. However, in Example 2 no diagonal W with positive elements can be found, such that $\sqrt{\det\hat{\Omega}_B}$ trace $W\hat{\Omega}_B$ is smaller than $\sqrt{\det\hat{\Omega}_A}$ trace $W\hat{\Omega}_A$. So neglect of the covariances would always result in worse forecasting performances here. Geometrically this means that the area of the unweighted forecasting ellips of model A is smaller than that of model B in both examples, although both times the circumscribed rectangle has a larger area in A. So the better forecasting performance of A would not appear when the forecasting intervals per variable were published, as Hymans (1968) proposes. So the choice of the model and the publication of the required forecasting interval must be separated.

4.2.3. *Inequality Coefficients*

To obtain a selection among models it is sometimes investigated what the forecasting performance of the models has been in a certain base period. Mostly the so-called inequalitycoefficients are used in doing so. There are several of them in use. Compared with the standard for selection presented here the inequality coefficients have the disadvantage that the extent to which the exogeneous variables in the forecasting period deviate from those in the reference period is not taken into account. Of course an evaluation of achieved forecasting results can also take place independent of the question with which model one should continue to make forecasts in future. One may ask e.g. whether the forecasting error remained indeed within the interval calculated. Apart from the fact that this can be caused by chance – when $\alpha=0.05$ on the average in one out of 20 cases – in case of a violation of the boundaries one will usually conclude that the model that was probable adequate for the reference period is no longer satisfactory for the forecasting period. Since it is never possible to trace a violation beforehand no standard for the choice of models can be derived from it.

In the literature ample attention has been paid to the evaluation of forecasting results [8]. The question which then comes to the front is which standard is the most suitable one for the evaluation. Strangely enough, one often rather considers the question how difficult it was to make the forecast than what the consequences have been of the forecasting errors made. The standard that fits in best with our criterion is the effectuated value of the loss-function $Z(\mathrm{e}_t)$. With a quadratic scalar function this becomes per period $Z_t=\mathrm{e}_t' W \mathrm{e}_t$, per variable $Z_i=\sum_t \mathrm{e}_{it}^2 W_i$ and for an overall evaluation $Z=\sum_t \mathrm{e}_t' W \mathrm{e}_t$.

Of course the actual problem is now what values must be substituted in W. With this much will depend on the specific content of $\mathbf{y}_t$, although general criteria are not impossible. E.g. if one states that in general damage caused by e_{it} is larger as y_{it} shows larger variances, and if one considers the joint behaviour of e_{it} and e_{jt} to be without damaging effects, then a good choice will be W diagonal with

$$W_i = \frac{1}{\sum_t y_{it}^2} \tag{4.19}$$

then Z becomes the inequality coefficient previously proposed by Theil (1954) and among others used by Verdoorn and van Eijk (1958) and by van den Beld (1965). The inequality coefficient later proposed by Theil (1958) would imply

$$W_i = \frac{1}{\sqrt{\sum_t y_{it}^2} + \sqrt{\sum_t \hat{y}_{it}^2}} \tag{4.20}$$

which has a much less clear meaning in this connection due to the presence of $\hat{y}_t$.

4.3. The Set of Models Considered and the Set of Admitted Models

4.3.1. *Introduction*

In the previous paragraph the composition of the criterion for selection has been analysed. In this paragraph it will be considered what the set of models consists of. The set considered in this book contains only models that can fit in with the classical regression model without restrictions on the coefficients. This limitation will be further elucidated in Subsection 4.3.2.

To what extent a considered model will be admitted depends on the degree in which the assumptions are tenable statistically. This is dealt with in Subsection 4.3.3. It will appear that when more alternative models are acknowledged the reaction on the testing will be different from the one in case of *one* model only.

4.3.2. *The Considered Set*

The models to which this book confines itself must satisfy the following conditions:

(1) $$\mathbf{y}_t = \Pi X_t + \mathbf{v}_t \tag{4.21}$$

in which $\mathbf{y}_t$ is an $m \times 1$ vector with the process variables,
Π is an $m \times k$ matrix with unknown parameters,
X_t is a $k \times 1$ vector with 'explanatory' variables,
$\mathbf{v}_t$ is an $m \times 1$ vector with disturbances $\mathbf{v}_{it}$.

(2) Observations must have been given for the past and as far as 'explanatory variables' are concerned, also for the future. So $\mathbf{y}_t$ for $t = 1, 2, \ldots, T$ and X_t for $T = 1, 2, \ldots, T$ and $t = \tau$.

(3) $$E\mathbf{v}_t = 0 \quad \text{for} \quad t = 1, 2, \ldots, T \quad \text{and} \quad t = \tau. \tag{4.22}$$

(4) $$\left.\begin{aligned} E\mathbf{v}_t\mathbf{v}'_{t^*} &= \Sigma \quad \text{for} \quad t = t^* \\ &= 0 \quad \text{for} \quad t \neq t^* \end{aligned}\right\} \quad \begin{aligned} &\text{for} \quad t = 1, 2, \ldots, T && (4.23\text{a}) \\ &\text{and} \quad t = \tau && (4.23\text{b}) \end{aligned}$$

(5) $X = [X'_{t-T}\, X'_{t-T+1} \ldots X'_{t-1}]$ is a $T \times k$ matrix of given values and rank $k \leqslant T$.

(6) $\mathbf{v}_t$ is normally distributed $t = 1, 2, \ldots, T$ and $t = \tau$.

We shall give a brief explanation about each of the assumptions.

Ad 1

Limitation to linear models was chosen in the first place as existing formulas could then be used. With linear models the forecasting error is also a linear function of the disturbance. In a one equation model e.g. the following holds for the vector of forecasting errors of the h years of the forecasting period.

$$\mathbf{e}_\tau = [I_\tau \quad - X'_t (X'X)^{-1} X'_\tau]\, \mathbf{v} \stackrel{\text{def}}{=} N\mathbf{v}$$

in which $\mathbf{v}$ is a vector with the $h+T$ disturbances of the future and the past and X_τ the $k \times h$ matrix with the values of the k exogeneous variables in each of the h years of the future.

For non-linear models N becomes dependent on $\mathbf{v}$, so that the moments of the distribution of $\mathbf{e}_\tau$ can, as a rule, only be expressed in higher moments of the distribution of $\mathbf{v}$. Requirements such as $E\mathbf{e}_\tau = 0$ are then impossible as long as $\mathbf{v}_t$ has a variance. And the variance of $\mathbf{e}_t$ will be of little use as a standard for selection, since it corresponds with the expectation of $\mathbf{v}$.

Moreover, a linear model is in the mean of the reference period a good approximation of a non-linear model if in a Taylor-expansion of the non-linear model the derivatives of order 2 and higher do not differ much from zero or if the deviations $X_{ji} - \bar{X}_j$ are small enough to neglect squares and products of these terms[9].

Since the discrepancies caused by the linear approach end up in the disturbances a linearization sometimes leads to higher values of det Σ and of its estimation det S. If some models of the set are in fact linear approximations of non-linear descriptions in any case least bad adjustments are chosen if we select according to det S – and consequently when θ and q are given also according to det $\theta\hat{\Omega}$.

Condition 1 also implies that the set remains restricted to the reduced forms of non-overidentified structure models, i.e. it has been assumed that there are no restrictions on the coefficients of (4.21).

Goldberger (1964, p. 365) remarks that estimations of Π that make use of the knowledge about the structural form can achieve more accurate forecasts. For, in that case more information is used which is expressed in the restrictions imposed on Π.

Goldberger, Nagar and Odeh (1961) have derived a consistent estimate of Ω, based on consistent estimations of the structural coefficients. They apply their method to Klein's small model for the U.S.A. In doing so they take the line that there exists only one possible form of the model generally written as

$$\Gamma \mathbf{y}_t + BX_t = \mathbf{u}_t . \tag{4.24}$$

If there would indeed be only one possible choice of $\Gamma \neq I$ and B, estimation of Π by way of P would not be allowed because of the neglection of the restrictions. However, the restrictions on Π become less important if it is possible to construct more models with the same variables but with different zerocoefficients in Γ and B. In fact, variations on Klein's model with the same $\mathbf{y}_t$ and X_t but with different Γ and B can also well be imagined.

So it is not unacceptable to limit the set to reduced forms in which there are no restrictions on the coefficients. It is a different matter whether one might arrive at lower estimates of det $\theta\Omega$ if the set of models is extended with all kinds of different structural forms for each reduced form. One might then select according to det $\theta\tilde{\Omega}$ in which $\tilde{\Omega}$ is the estimate of Ω according to Goldberger *et al.* That possibility has not been investigated in this book. Since the calculations for Goldberger's formula are rather extensive, the emphasis in the selection might sooner be put on the zero coefficients in Π than on a selection of exogeneous variables. I have the impression that the latter method provides often more possibilities for variation, especially in case of forecasting periods of only one time-unit. So concentration on the optimal reduced forms, without taking account of the restrictions, seems to be a good starting point.

Finally, with condition ad 1 linear models in transformations of $\mathbf{y}_t$ are also excluded. Of course, it is in itself possible first to make a forecast of the variable $\mathbf{z}_t = f(\mathbf{y}_t)$ by way of a linear model and afterwards to transform $\mathbf{z}_t$ again in $\mathbf{y}_t$. Then one has in fact still a model in $\mathbf{y}_t$ by way of $f^{-1}(\mathbf{z}_t)$. If e.g. $f(\mathbf{y}_t) = \ln \mathbf{y}_t$ that model is not linear in $\mathbf{v}_t$ and consequently is not discussed here. If $f(\mathbf{y}_t) = \Delta\mathbf{y}_t$ the model is indeed linear in $\mathbf{y}_t$ but no more admitted, because a linear model in $\Delta\mathbf{y}_t$ implies for $\mathbf{y}_t$ a matrix with *a priori* coefficients. For, if the model is

$$\Delta\mathbf{y}_t = \Pi^* X_t + \mathbf{v}_t$$

we have

$$\mathbf{y}_t = [I \quad \Pi^*] \begin{bmatrix} \mathbf{y}_{t-1} \\ X_t \end{bmatrix} + \mathbf{v}_t .$$

Instead of the model that contains a matrix with *a priori* coefficients one can write more generally

$$\mathbf{y}_t = [A \quad \Pi^*] \begin{bmatrix} \mathbf{y}_{t-1} \\ X_t \end{bmatrix} + \mathbf{v}_t$$

with an unknown matrix of coefficients A. The latter model will be admitted here in as far as the values of $\mathbf{y}_{t-1}$ are already known, so for y_{t-1}. See further Section 4.5 for the problem of the lagged process variables.

Ad 2

This restriction has been mentioned before (see Section 2.2). If there are no observations there is no connection between model and reality. If the values of the exogeneous variables for the future are lacking the connection between model and reality is useless.

Ad 3

This can be written in combination with ad 1 as

$$E\mathbf{y}_t = \Pi X_t \quad \text{for} \quad t = 1, 2, \ldots, T \quad \text{and} \quad t = \tau .$$

Ad 4

Assumption (4.23b) implies that no autocorrelation has been admitted. One might make more general assumptions here with respect to the matrix $\mathscr{V}(\boldsymbol{\varepsilon})$[10] instead of starting from $\Psi = \Sigma \otimes I_T$, but it is not possible to start from a fully unknown $\mathscr{V}(\boldsymbol{\varepsilon})$, because then there are too many parameters to be able to estimate this $\mathscr{V}(\boldsymbol{\varepsilon})$. Accordingly a purely empirical theory is not possible. One shall have to choose certain parameters of $\mathscr{V}(\boldsymbol{\varepsilon})$ *a priori*. It seems plausible to give first the value 0 to the autocorrelation coefficients of higher order, so starting with the bottom left element of $\mathscr{V}(\boldsymbol{\varepsilon})$ and so on. When attributing *a priori* coefficients one should at least continue until the problem of estimation has become solvable. It is usually possible to define such a model thus that there is no autocorrelation left. Of course in an actual situation it must be tested whether the absence of any autocorrelation is a justified assumption. This is dealt with in Subsection 4.3.3.

To what extent the set of models is restricted to models with autocorrelation will become apparent when all models with autocorrelation are formulated in transformations of $\mathbf{y}_t$ without autocorrelation. Such a transformation of $\mathbf{y}_t$ is usual in generalized least squares estimations. The transformed variable is then a linear function of $\mathbf{y}_t$ and of lagged values of $\mathbf{y}_t$. If one compares the latter specification with a model in which lagged values of $\mathbf{y}_t$ have been included in the explanatory vector X_t, the difference is that in the former specification restrictions on the coefficients must be taken into account.

With this a situation has arisen that can be compared with the one discussed under ad 1, when using structural forms. Usually a model with the same explanatory variables without restrictions on the coefficients is also acceptable. This is then a good starting-point. This book is limited to the latter kind of models. So it does not enter into the question to what extent the introduction of restrictions leads to better forecasts. The result of such an introduction is not certain beforehand. It depends on the fact whether an inferior adjustment due to the restrictions is compensated for by the greater number of degrees of freedom.

Because of (4.23a) assumption ad 4 also implies homoskedasticity. With respect to this the same holds as for autocorrelation, to this effect that with a complete variable Σ_t estimation becomes impossible. One shall at least have to adopt a function for Σ_t that permits estimation with T observations. Then a homoskedastic alternative in transformed variables can always be formulated. However, as it has been remarked under ad 1, models in transformations of $\mathbf{y}_t$ will not be discussed here.

Ad 5

The explanatory variables are limited to variables for which the values of the forecasting period can be determined with certainty. It is important to go into this point more in detail, the more so because the choice of the explanatory variables determines the difference between the models. So the number of models that is considered depends on the number of different specifications of the vector X_t.

Well, what variables can be admitted in X_t? In principle each variable for which T observations in the reference period are available, and for which the value in the forecasting period is also known. So all lagged variables with a lag smaller than the forecasting period fail as useful explanatory variables. So in case of the forecast of $\mathbf{y}_{t+\tau}$ this is extended to all variables with a lag smaller than τ. Variables that are considered to be exogeneous by economists but the value of which is not known beforehand, such as the growth of the population, world trade, government expenses are equally excluded.

In fact only functions of time are admitted, or lagged and known variables (both endogeneous and exogeneous variables) if the forecasting period is not longer than the lag. In fact still a very large number of variables come under this definition. This can best be illustrated with an example. Let us assume that it is discovered that during a large number of years the export surplus in The Netherlands has run parallel to the average summer temperature in N.S. Wales in the previous year. Let us also assume that this temperature is known fast enough to enable people to base a forecast on it Then assume that there exists also an economic theory explaining the export surplus of The Netherlands yet which does not achieve such precision in the description of the reference period that as a result the forecasting interval for the export suplus becomes smaller than the interval based on the 'accidental' relation with the summer temperature in N.S. Wales.

Which specification would one choose for a *forecast*? With this it must be stated clearly that the point is not whether the explanation for the existence of the relation is in itself sufficiently satisfying, but merely whether it can be made acceptable that the relation found will also be valid in the forecasting period. In my opinion no objective unambiguous criterion can be given for the plausibility of the continuation of a relation. It cannot be decided to what extent the economic relation is more reliable for the forecasting period than the 'accidental' one. In order yet to arrive at a uniform approach we shall therefore only apply the standard of the 'empirical' evidence. To this it should be added immediately that it will not be simple to find a good 'accidental' relation that gives a small forecasting interval. So one might have to search for a long time, certainly if the vector $\mathbf{y}_t$ contains more than 1 component. So it is much more useful to limit oneself in the searching to (groups of) variables of which it is *a priori* expected that they will help to create a small forecasting interval. There are three such groups of variables:

(a) Functions of time.

This is based on the idea that economic timeseries show certain regular features in their development through time. One usually decomposes series into trend, business cycle and seasonal movements.

(b) Lagged process variables.

The use of these variables is in fact based on the same idea as given in a. For, if one writes $\mathbf{y}_t$ as a (linear) function of $\mathbf{y}_{t-1}, \mathbf{y}_{t-2}, \ldots, \mathbf{y}_{t-p}$ we get a difference equation of the order p, the solution of which presents $\mathbf{y}_t$ as a function of time.

The variables under (b) and, in a wider sense, also those under (a) are the forecasting instruments of the 'controllers', although they usually do not estimate the coefficients[11].

(c) Variables that are suggested by economic theory.

Naturally economic theory will often appoint a combination of variables as explanatory factors, but one is not committed to this combination. Neither must variables under (a), (b) and (c) be regarded as exclusive groups.

In this context it is useful to draw attention to the practice of economic forecasting. As regards the choice of the explanatory variables one takes a somewhat less strict line. In most empirical models also unlagged variables are admitted as explanatory variables. It is assumed then that their values for the forecasting period can be given quite accurately. One gives in fact conditional forecasts, the condition being the correctness of the value of the exogeneous variables in the forecasting period. Feldstein (1971) tries to meet this problem by incorporating the stochasticity of the exogeneous variables in the formulas for the forecasting interval by way of a subjective variance-covariance matrix. Then the variance of the forecasting error becomes, if $\mathbf{y}_t$ is a scalar ($m=1$)

$$Ee_\tau^2 = \hat{\boldsymbol{\beta}}'\Xi\hat{\boldsymbol{\beta}} + \text{trace } \Xi\Phi + \mathbf{X}_\tau'\Phi\mathbf{X}_\tau + \sigma^2 \tag{4.25}$$

in which Φ and Ξ are respectively the variance-covariance matrices of the regressioncoefficients $\hat{\boldsymbol{\beta}}$ and the variables $\mathbf{X}_t$. If Ξ is replaced by the a priori value $\tilde{\Xi}$ and σ^2 and Φ respectively by the estimates s^2 and $s^2(X'X)^{-1}$ obtained by applying least squares, then the estimated variance of the forecasting error becomes

$$\hat{\Omega} = s^2 [\mathbf{X}_\tau'(X'X)^{-1}\mathbf{X}_\tau + \text{trace } (X'X)^{-1}\tilde{\Xi} + 1] + \hat{\boldsymbol{\beta}}'\tilde{\Xi}\hat{\boldsymbol{\beta}}. \tag{4.26}$$

Going on this way one could also adjust the standard det $\hat{\Omega}$ for models with $m>1$. As a matter of fact Feldstein gives formulas to do this. When using them one approaches a Bayesian analysis, as Feldstein indeed admits.

It is obvious that the selection will be influenced if subjective variance-covariance matrices are admitted. Then a model might be chosen by means of a 'favourable' forecast of the values of the exogeneous variables, i.e. values X_τ close to the mean $\bar{X}$. If the 'favourable' value is in fact a coloured representation the model might be chosen unjustly. In this book we have taken the line throughout that there exists no *a priori* knowledge about the parameters of the distributions. So we shall only admit non-stochastic explanatory variables, in other words only that X_t for which $\tilde{\Xi}=0$. If this value is filled in in (4.26) then (3.39) follows with $S=s^2$.

A *conditional forecast* is certainly possible as an intermediate phase, namely not only if one wishes to investigate to what extent knowledge about the value of a variable in the forecasting period might contribute to the forecast, but it is often also possible to trace better models this way. For if a suitable method is found to predict the 'conditioned' variables this may sometimes lead to a better forecasting procedure of the variable required. So starting a forecasting procedure by looking for good conditional forecasts is a matter of efficiency in the searching for suitable explanatory variables. For this see the examples $Q\,[Q_{-1}\,\mathbf{b}_c]$ and $Q\,[Q_{-1}\,\tilde{\mathbf{w}}]$ in Chapter V.

Ad 6

The assumption that $\mathbf{v}_t$ is normally distributed will mostly be acceptable, especially in macro-economic models, on the basis of the Central Limit Theorem. A more general approach of the selection might start from Tchebycheff-intervals, as e.g. Feldstein does. This has as a disadvantage that it is not easy to find the connection with the selection procedure. For this 'a single quantity' is needed. Moreover, the Tchebycheff-intervals are often so wide that they have little appeal. Then $\det \hat{\Omega}$ would even be preferable as a standard so without θ. The selection would then turn out a little more favourable for models with normally distributed $\mathbf{v}_t$ and many exogeneous variables.

4.3.3. *The Set of Admitted Models*

In 4.3.2 a description has been given of the set of models to which this book extends. This section elucidates which part of it should be disregarded for being unrealistic. A model that formally satisfies the previously mentioned conditions 1–6 inc., yet the assumptions of which are not tenable given the observations, cannot be admitted to the set. In the concrete this means that a model will be admitted as long as it has not been proved by way of a statistical test that the assumptions are in conflict with the observations.

Before discussing the testing procedure we must answer the fundamental question whether testing a model is still necessary if it is only used in applications. Some are of the opinion that applications require only the estimation of coefficients in aprioristic ideas. This cannot be defended on the ground that estimation is possible even when testing has become impossible. Surely, as soon as a number of assumptions has been made, sufficient to solve the estimation problem, some assumptions can usually be tested as well. This holds e.g. for the estimation of the forecasting interval. As soon as a sufficient number of assumptions has been made to calculate this, a test on (4.23) or (4.21) can be carried out equally well. Omitting this possible way of testing may be criticised with Tinbergen (1956, p. 32):

Propositions derived from aprioristic models have proved to be dangerous, primarily because so many aprioristic models are not realistic.

Consequently, a model will not be admitted here if it is not possible to test it in any way.

Since the said assumptions 1–6 inc. are mutually independent it would be desirable to test each of them separately. In this way it could be decided which of these assumptions form a reliable startingpoint for an admitted model. However, an independent test per assumption is not possible. The testing of each assumption is conditional to this extent that some assumptions are accepted as valid when others are being tested. In other words, the complete set of assumptions can only be tested as a whole, or, as Neyman and Pearson (1967, p. 1) point out: Testing stochastic theories is testing 'whether or not a particular sample may be judged as likely to have been randomly drawn from a certain population, whose form may be either completely or only partly specified'. If on the basis of certain test statistics it becomes improbable in whatsoever way that the observed sample has been drawn from the described population, the whole model, i.e. the complex of assumptions will be rejected. This implies that *all* models should be tested on as many aspects as possible.

In the framework of this book testing on (4.21) and (4.22) adopts a character of its own. It also appears that our method will have consequences for the testing on (4.23). The testing on the other aspects does not differ from the usual method. The testing on the assumption ad 2 is trivial, the one ad 5 has been sufficiently explained in Subsection 4.3.2. However, some comment is desirable on the testing of the remaining assumptions.

Ad 6

In the testing on normality it is shown clearly that it is not possible to test the assumptions independently. The assumption that $\mathbf{v}_t$ is normally distributed can only be tested if it is assumed that $\mathbf{v}_t$ and $\mathbf{v}_{t*}$ with $t \neq t^*$ are independently distributed and that consequently autocorrelation does not occur. On the other hand, autocorrelation cannot be tested if no assumption has made about the distribution of the disturbance. So the absence of autocorrelation can be tested given the normality proposition and vice versa. We choose the first possibility because on the basis of the Central Limit Theorem it can be made plausible that in macro-economic models 6 is usually satisfied.

Ad 1, Ad 3 and Ad 4

Since (4.21) is a definition equation of $\mathbf{v}_t$ the issue in ad 1 and ad 3 together is actually a test whether the hypothesis

$$E\mathbf{y}_t = \Pi X_t \tag{4.27}$$

may be adopted. So, in combination with ad 4, two tests are possible for each model, the one on (4.23) and the one on (4.27)[12]. One should bear in mind that this test adopts a special character here because there is not merely one alternative hypothesis, but we have a whole series of them.

We shall illustrate the underlying principles by way of models with one equation only. The set considered in this book is characterised by the fact that all models included in it differ only in the specification of (4.21). This results in the following picture

$$\begin{array}{ll}
\text{(a)} & \mathbf{y}_t = \beta_0 + \beta_1 X_{1t} + \beta_2 X_{2t} + \mathbf{v}_t \\
\text{(b)} & \mathbf{y}_t = \beta_0 + \beta_1 X_{1t} \qquad\qquad + \mathbf{v}_t \\
\text{(c)} & \mathbf{y}_t = \beta_0 + \qquad\quad \beta_2 X_{2t} + \mathbf{v}_t \\
\text{(d)} & \mathbf{y}_t = \qquad \beta_1 X_{1t} + \beta_2 X_{2t} + \mathbf{v}_t \\
\text{(e)} & \mathbf{y}_t = \beta_0 \qquad\qquad\qquad\quad + \mathbf{v}_t \\
\text{(f)} & \mathbf{y}_t = \qquad \beta_1 X_{1t} \qquad\qquad + \mathbf{v}_t \\
\text{(g)} & \mathbf{y}_t = \qquad\qquad\qquad \beta_2 X_{2t} + \mathbf{v}_t \\
\text{(h)} & \mathbf{y}_t = \qquad\qquad\qquad\qquad\quad + \mathbf{v}_t
\end{array} \tag{4.28}$$

$$\mathbf{y}_t = \gamma_0 + \gamma_1 X_{3t} + \gamma_2 X_{4t} + u_t \tag{4.29}$$

etc., etc.

When a coefficient β_j is specified, this means that it is different from 0. E.g. for (4.28a) β_0 β_1 and β_2 are different from 0 ex hypothesis.

We can formulate all this more precisely with the help of the following definitions:

D is a set with all considered variables X_{rt}, $r=1, 2, \ldots, K$.

$S(s)$ is a linear specification – like (4.28c) – of the equation which describes

$\mathbf{y}_t$ as a function of s explanatory variables X_{jt}, $j=1, 2, \ldots, s$, in which X_{jt} belongs to D.

$S(K)$ is called a *maximumspecification.*

If $T<K-1$ where T represents the number of observations, estimation of σ^2 in $S(K)$ is not possible and consequently, neither is testing of 0 coefficients or estimation of the forecasting interval. According to our starting-points the maximumspecification is not admissable then and neither are all $S(s)$ for which $T<s-1$. In that case we form all $\binom{K}{T-1}$ different specifications $S(T-1)$. We indicate them by $S_i(T-1)$, $i=1, 2, \ldots, \binom{K}{T-1}$.

$S_i(T-1)$ is called a *truncated maximumspecification* (belonging to group i). Group i is a subset of D containing a choice of $T-1$ variables X_s from D.

We shall now discuss

(1) The testing of $S(K)$ if $K<T-1$.
(2) The testing of $S(s)$ if $K<T-1$.
(3) The testing of $S_i(T-1)$ if $K\geqslant T-1$.
(4) The testing of $S_i(s)$ if $K\geqslant T-1$.

(1) *The testing of* $S(K)$

If $K<T-1$ we can estimate the parameters of the maximumspecification and also the forecasting interval belonging to $S(K)$. The maximum-specification is not admitted if the assumption $\beta_j=0$ for $j>K$ is not valid. It is only possible to test this if it is indicated which variable X_j has been omitted. This variable is no part of D per definition. With respect to this we can hardly do anything else but what is usual in dealing with only 1 model, i.e. to assume that the specification $S(K)$ is not incorrect until the contrary has been proved. This is only possible through ex-tension of D. So our conclusion is that the coefficients of a maximum-specification are not tested. Yet the model which includes this specification must be tested on (4.23). This is divided in a test on the absence of auto-correlation (4.23b) and a test on homoskedasticity (4.23a). As we know, the difficulty in this test lies in the fact that the least squares residuals $\hat{\mathbf{v}}_{it}$

are not independently distributed, even if the disturbances $\mathbf{v}_{it}$ are. Nevertheless, various testingprocedures have been designed in case of only 1 endogeneous variable ($m=1$). These procedures aim for the larger part at testing on autocorrelation, although, for testing on homoskedasticity we also know some teststatistics[13].

If $m>1$ additional difficulties arise since autocorrelation in one of the series of the disturbances is removed to the other disturbances by way of the coherence in (4.23a). Testing on autocorrelation of one of the disturbances $\mathbf{v}_{it}$ is insufficient, testing on each of the disturbances separately, so $i=1, 2, \ldots, m$ fails to appreciate (4.23a). I know of no solution from the literature.

However, our set-up also sheds a different light on the testing of (4.23b), if $m=1$. We shall test on autocorrelation according to Durbin and Watson's widely used boundstests (1951). As we know, for the testing against positive autocorrelation Durbin and Watson's tables (1951) give two critical values for the teststatistic **d**, a lower limit d_L and an upper limit d_U. Between those two there is an 'inconclusive region' for which no statistical conclusions can be drawn. In Chapter V as a first approach we shall only deal with the values d_L or $4-d_L$ for the testing on negative autocorrelation, i.e. we shall reject a model (of 1 equation) if $d<d_L$ or $d>4-d_L$ and we shall not reject it in the other cases. A more complete set-up should be supplemented by another teststatistic for the situation $d_L \leqslant d \leqslant d_U$. However, there is yet another difficulty. Durbin and Watson's testprocedure has been designed for specifications with a small number of explanatory variables. Durbin and Watson's tables (1951) do not go any further than $K=6$ (including the constant). However, with a maximumspecification K is usually much larger. Of course this also holds good for testing on autocorrelation of all $S(s)$ and $S_i(s)$ where s is large. Moreover, with increasing K or s the 'inconclusive region' becomes rapidly larger. Koerts and Abrahamse (1969) discuss the situation of specifications with a small number of degrees of freedom and they propose in such cases either to use the BLUS-estimates or the exact significance limits of the Durbin-Watson statistic for the given values of the exogeneous variables, which is of course much more laborious than the use of the boundstests. Therefore the latter is still recommended in case of a large number of degrees of freedom.

More recently Abrahamse and Koerts (1971) developed a new estimate of the residuals. According to them a test can be constructed with this estimate which has a higher power than the BLUS- or Durbin-Watson statistics. A similar test can also be calculated for low values of $T-K$, probably even for the situation $T-K=1$, which we shall meet hereafter. It remains to be investigated to what extent it is possible to build these testprocedures efficiently into the selection. It has already been found that testing by way of comparison of the Durbin-Watson d with the bound d_L or $4-d_L$ does not lead to difficulties in this respect. If the test-procedure is extended, a test on homoskedasticity can also be built in, if necessary.

(2) *The testing of $S(s)$*

$S(s)$ differs from $S(K)$ because in $S(s)$ one coefficient or more have been put equal to 0. When we want to indicate which coefficients we write $S(s; h_1, h_2, \ldots, h_{K-s})$. Testing of the zerocoefficients can take place on the ground of all specifications $S(r)$ with $s+1 \leqslant r \leqslant K$, that contain the same X_j as $S(s)$. If $r=s+1$, this takes place on the basis of a t-test or an $F(1, T-k)$-test on the zerocoefficient of $S(s)$ in question. If $r>s+1$ this takes place on the basis of an $F(j, T-k)$-test on j zerocoefficients.

Testing of the zerocoefficients of $S(s)$ on the basis of $S(r)$ is only admitted if $S(r)$ itself has been admitted. This implies that the testingprocedure starts with testing of $S(K)$ on autocorrelation, etc.[14] If $S(K)$ has been admitted, the zerocoefficients of all $S(k-1; j)$ $j=1, 2, \ldots, K$ are tested. All *admitted* $S(K-1;j)$ are then tested on autocorrelation, etc. The $S(K-1;j)$ that have been admitted form also in this respect the basis for the testing of $S(K-2;j, h)$ etc. If $S(K)$ is not admitted, the test on the zerocoefficients of $S(K-1;j)$ is abandoned. We assume then that each $S(K-1;j)$ has been admitted in this respect and we continue with the testing of all K specifications $S(K-1;j)$ on autocorrelation, etc. If one of them has not been admitted this $S(K-1;j)$ is also abandoned as a basis for the testing on the zerocoefficients of $S(K-2;j, h)$. If ($S(K)$, $S(K-1; j)$ and $S(K-1, h)$ have all been admitted, $S(K-2;j, h)$ can be tested with the help of a t-test on the basis of $S(K-1;j)$ or $S(K-1; h)$ or with the help of an $F(2, T-k)$-test on the basis of $S(K)$. For an arbitrary $S(s)$ we now have the following possibilities:

$K-s$ $\quad$ t or $F(1, T-k)$-tests on the basis of $S(s+1)$;

$\binom{K-s}{2}$ $F(2, T-k)$-tests on the basis of $S(s+2)$
etc., etc. until

1 $F(K-s, T-k)$-test on the basis of $S(K)$.

When some $S(r)$ with $s+1 \leqslant r \leqslant K$ have not been admitted, the number of possibilities for testing becomes smaller. The following situations may occur when $S(s)$ is tested on the basis of $S(r_1)$ and $S(r_2)$ with $s+1 \leqslant r_i \leqslant K$ for $i=1, 2, \ldots$

	admitted	not admitted
admitted	(1) $S(s)$ is admitted on the basis of $S(r_1)$ *and* $S(r_2)$.	(2) $S(s)$ is admitted on the basis of $S(r_1)$ but not according to $S(r_2)$.
not admitted	(3) $S(s)$ is admitted on the basis of $S(r_2)$ but not according to $S(r_1)$.	(4) $S(s)$ is neither admitted according to $S(r_2)$ nor according to $S(r_1)$.

We shall only admit $S(s)$ in case (1). This means that $S(s)$ is not admitted if at least one $S(r)$ can be found, such that $S(s)$ is not admitted. So in general it is not necessary to perform *all* tests on *each* $S(s)$. If $S(s)$ has proved to be inadmissable it is not necessary to perform any further tests. What lines one wiskes to take in the test procedure is also dependent on the size of K. In general one should arrange the procedure in such a way that the non-admitted models are excluded with as little calculation as possible. If K is small, it seems to be more efficient first to check each $S(s)$ on its having been admitted on the basis of $S(s+1)$, then to test the not yet rejected $S(s)$ on autocorrelation, etc. and only afterwards to test on the basis of $S(s+2)$, $S(s+3)$ etc., if necessary. If K is large the following set-up seems to be more appropriate:

(1) Call the set of admitted, respectively non-admitted specifications $\mathscr{T}$ and $\mathscr{N}$.

(2) Test $S(K)$ on autocorrelation etc. In our calculations this was done by comparing d with d_L respectively $4-d_L$. This must be revised, respectively adapted for smaller values of $T-k$ and values of d in the

'inconclusive region'. If $S(K)$ has been admitted, include it in $\mathcal{T}$ and continue with item (3). If $S(K)$ has not been admitted, include it in $\mathcal{N}$ and continue with item (6).

(3) Test each $S(K-1;j)$ on the basis of $S(K)$ to see whether $\beta_j = 0$ is admitted. This is done with a t-test.[15]

(4) Include the specifications that have not been admitted on account of item (3) in $\mathcal{N}$. Assume there are l of them. Choose the indices in such a way that these specifications can be written as $S(K-1, 1)$ $S(K-1, 2)$, ..., $S(K-1; l)$.

(5) We now have the following situation

$S(K-1;1)\ldots S(K-1,l)$	$S(K-1,l+1)\ldots S(K-1;K)$
$\downarrow$	$\downarrow$
non-admitted on the basis of (4).	see item (6).

In order to judge the admissability of e.g. $S(K-2; 1, 2)$ or $S(K-4; 2, 3, 4, 9)$ etc. one investigates on the basis of $S(K)$ with the help of an F-test the admissibility of all specifications that proceed from $S(K)$ through the elimination of 2 or more of the l variables mentioned.

So we test

$\binom{l}{2}$ specifications $S(K-2; i, j) \quad i, j = 1, 2, \ldots, l \quad i \neq j.$

$\binom{l}{3}$ specifications $S(K-3; i, j, h) \quad i, j, h = 1, 2, \ldots, l \quad i \neq j \neq h.$

1 specification $S(K-1; 1, 2, \ldots, l).$

All specifications that are not admitted are included in $\mathcal{N}$.

(6) Test every $S(K-1)$ that has not yet been included in $\mathcal{N}$ on autocorrelation. If there is no significant autocorrelation $S(K-1)$ is included in $\mathcal{T}$, and otherwise in $\mathcal{N}$.

(7) Have all $S(K-1)$ included in $\mathcal{T}$ form the basis for a test on the the $S(K-2)$ that are derived from these $S(K-1)$ and that have not yet been included in $\mathcal{N}$. This test is again a t-test.

(8) Include the $S(K-2)$ not admitted on account of item (7) in $\mathcal{N}$. Repeat the procedure as described for $S(K-1)$ in (4) and (5) for each of these bases $S(K-2)$.

(9) Test the $S(K-2)$ that have not yet been admitted in $\mathscr{N}$ on autocorrelation, etc.

(10) Continue this procedure until each model has been tested on its coefficients or on autocorrelation (or on both).

The set $\mathscr{T}$ that has thus been obtained may still contain models that should be non-admitted according to our rules. For in the program of 10 items the rigorous testing described at the beginning of this passage Ad 2 has not been executed. If few models remain in $\mathscr{T}$ one might perhaps investigate which of their $S(s)$ have not yet been tested on $S(r)$ with $r > s+1$ and one might perform this test as yet.

In this procedure we still have the problem of meeting specifications without a constant term. The test-statistic calculated by Durbin and Watson cannot directly be applied to regressions through the origin. According to Kramer (1970) critical regions for this situation can be derived in the same way. Kramer gives tables for $T \geqslant 10$ and $1 \leqslant K \leqslant 6$, in which the K does not cover the constant term.

(3) *The testing of* $S_i(T-1)$

The testing of $S_i(T-1)$ takes place in the same way as the one of $S(K)$. However, there is a difference. For, with constant T we can never find an X_j such that $S_i(T-1)$ is not admitted on the basis of zerocoefficients. Only when we get 1 additional observation of y_t and all X_t there are $\binom{K}{T}$ new specifications $S_i(T-1)$ that can be tested on a zerocoefficient.

The fact that $S_i(T-1)$ has only 1 degree of freedom makes the problem of testing on autocorrelation, as discussed before, most to the point. So for this situation we shall not be able to use the Durbin-Watson boundstest, but we shall have to change to one of the other testing-procedures, mentioned before.

(4) *The testing of* $S_i(s)$

The testing of $S_i(s)$ takes place inside the group of specifications belonging to $S_i(T-1)$ just as it happens with the testing of $S(s)$ inside the one group that can be derived from $S(K)$ with one exception. It is of course possible and it happens frequently that $S_i(s)$ is the same specification as $S_j(s)$. The latter belongs to a different group and has been derived from a different truncated maximumspecification. Finally, we only admit $S_i(s)$

to $\mathscr{T}$, if it has not been removed to the set $\mathscr{N}$ in any group.

I propose the following procedure to build up the admitted set of models:

(1) Collect K variables belonging to one of the three groups mentioned on p. 62

(2) If $K \geqslant T$ form $\binom{K}{T-1}$ maximumspecifications.

(3) Apply the test procedure, as described in the 10 items on p. 71 and 72 to $S(K)$ or all $S_i(T-1)$.

(4) The result of this procedure is the admitted set $\mathscr{T}$ of specifications that can neither be rejected because of their coefficients nor because of autocorrelation.

4.3.4. *Selection in Case of More Equations*

The former procedures can also be applied to models with more equations. In doing so there are two difficulties:

(a) No test on autocorrelation is available yet in case of $m > 1$.

(b) Even when the equations contain the same *number* of exogeneous variables, but the exogeneous variables are not the same ones in all equations, the optimal forecasting procedure no longer equals the least squares estimate per equation. Then the optimal testing of the models requires roundabout calculations in 2 stages[16].

In connection with (b) we shall restrict ourselves to selection of models with the same exogeneous variables for all equations. In doing so we shall have to accept the maximumspecification or – if $T > K + m - 1$ – the truncated maximumspecifications without testing, this contrary to our fundamental rules, as long as no simultaneous test on autocorrelation exists. The test on the elimination of a variable then takes place, based on the following.

Let Y be the $T \times m$ matrix of observations of the m variables to be explained[17], and X_k the $T \times k$ matrix of observations of the variables to be explained, then

$$(E'E)_k = Y'Y - Y'X_k(X_k'X_k)^{-1} X_k'Y \tag{4.30}$$

is the $m \times m$ matrix of sums of squares of the residuals, if there are k explanatory variables.

Assume

$$\hat{\Sigma}_k = \frac{(E'E)_k}{T}\ ^{18}$$

and define

$$U_{m,1,T-k} = \frac{\det \hat{\Sigma}_k}{\det \hat{\Sigma}_{k-1}} \tag{4.31}$$

According to Anderson (1958, p. 195, Theorem 8.5.3) the magnitude

$$\frac{1 - U_{m,1,T-k}}{U_{m,1,T-k}} \frac{T-k-m+1}{m} \tag{4.32}$$

has an F-distribution with m and $T-k-m+1$ degrees of freedom.

In the next section[19] we shall see that

$$\frac{\det \hat{\Sigma}_k}{\det \hat{\Sigma}_{k-1}} = \frac{\det (E'E)_k}{\det (E\ E)_{k-1}} = \frac{1}{1 + P'_{i\cdot}[r(E'E)_k]^{-1} P_{\cdot i}} \tag{4.33}$$

in which $P_{\cdot i}$ is the column of regressioncoefficients belonging to the variable X_i to be eliminated and $r = (X'_k X_k)^{-1}_{ii}$ the element ii from $(X'_k X_k)^{-1}$. When we now substitute (4.33) through (4.31) in (4.32) it appears that the teststatistic (4.32) can be written as

$$\frac{T-k-m+1}{m} P'_{i\cdot}[r(E'E)_k]^{-1} P_{\cdot i}. \tag{4.34}$$

For diagonal $(E'E)_k$ (4.34) is the sum of the squares of the student-t variables of the regressioncoefficients involved. In other words: for diagonal $(E'E)_k$ (4.34) becomes

$$\sum_{j=1}^{k} \frac{1}{\xi_{ij}^2}$$

in which ξ_{ij} is the relative standard error of the element P_{ij} of P.

4.4. Efficiency in the Selection of the Optimal Forecasting Procedure

4.4.1. *Introduction*

It has been described in the previous paragraph in what way it can be decided whether a linear stochastic model is admitted. For the non-maximum specifications the admission takes place only after a test on the tenability of the specification of the equations. In the first step $S(s)$ was tested on the basis of $S(s+1)$ with $s<K$ or $s<T-1$. It can now be demonstrated that, sometimes, one can immediately tell from the test-statistics

$$\mathbf{t}_{b_i} = \frac{1}{\xi_i} \quad \text{for } m = 1 \quad \text{and} \quad P'_{i}.(rE'E_k)^{-1} P._i \quad \text{for } m > 1$$

that the forecasting interval of the model in question is always larger than that of another specification from $\mathscr{T}$. This is laid down in a number of lemma's in Subsections 4.4.2 and 4.4.3.

4.4.2. *One Equation*

Let *model A* be defined as

$$\mathbf{y} = X\beta + \mathbf{u}$$

in which $\mathbf{y}$ is a vector with length T,
X is a $T\times k$ matrix of given values with rank k,
$\mathbf{u}$ is a random drawing from a multivariate normal distribution with $E\mathbf{u}=0$ and $E\mathbf{uu}'=\sigma^2 I_T$.

Assume A has been admitted.

Let *model B* be defined as

$$\mathbf{y} = X_1\beta_1 + \mathbf{u}_1$$

in which X_1 is a $T\times(k-1)$ submatrix of X with rank $k-1$, obtained by the elimination of column X_i from X.
Moreover $E\mathbf{u}_1=0$ and $E\mathbf{u}_1\mathbf{u}_1'=\sigma_1^2 I_T$.

In model B the parameter β_i is assumed to be zero. To what extent this is correct can be tested statistically with the help of $\mathbf{b}_i$, the least squares estimator of β_i in A and $\mathbf{s}_{b_i}$, the standard error of b_i. The hypothesis $\beta_i=0$ is rejected if

$$|t_{b_i}| = \frac{|b_i|}{s_{b_i}} = \frac{1}{\xi_i} \geqslant t_\alpha$$

with given α.

As is well known, $\mathbf{t}_{b_i}$ has a student-t distribution with $T-k$ degrees of freedom.

If $|t_{b_i}| < t_\alpha$, model B is *admitted* just as model A. Which of the two models A and B is chosen in this case depends on the criterion $\det \theta\hat{\Omega}$. It can be proved that the criterion for selection will turn out in favour of B if $|t_{b_i}| \leqslant 1$. This implies that in such a case it is not necessary to collect information about the values of X_{it} in the forecasting period. We then call model B relevant. To give the proof of the statement we derive the following lemma's.

LEMMA 3

For the estimated variances s_k and s_{k-1} of the models A and B the following is true.

$$\begin{aligned} s_{k-1}^2 &< s_k^2 \quad \text{if and only if} \quad |t_{b_i}| < 1 \\ s_{k-1}^2 &= s_k^2 \quad \text{if and only if} \quad |t_{b_i}| = 1 \\ s_{k-1}^2 &> s_k^2 \quad \text{if and only if} \quad |t_{b_i}| > 1 . \end{aligned}$$

Proof

Form

$$A = \begin{bmatrix} y'y & y'X \\ X'y & X'X \end{bmatrix} \quad \text{and} \quad A_1 = \begin{bmatrix} y'y & y'X_1 \\ X'y & X_1'X_1 \end{bmatrix} .$$

According to Graybill (1961, p. 9)

$$\det A = \det(y'y - y'X(X'X)^{-1} X'y) \cdot \det X'X = \\ = (\mathrm{e}'\mathrm{e})_k \det X'X .$$

So

$$(\mathrm{e}'\mathrm{e})_k = \frac{\det A}{\det X'X} \quad \text{and} \quad (\mathrm{e}'\mathrm{e})_{k-1} = \frac{\det A_1}{\det X_1'X_1}$$

and consequently

$$\frac{(\mathrm{e}'\mathrm{e})_{k-1}}{(\mathrm{e}'\mathrm{e})_k} = \frac{\det A_1}{\det A} \frac{\det X'X}{\det X_1'X_1} = \frac{A_{i+1,\,i+1}^{-1}}{(X'X)_{ii}^{-1}} \tag{4.35}$$

in which $(X'X)_{ii}^{-1}$ and $A_{i+1,\,i+1}^{-1}$ form respectively the element ii of $(X'X)^{-1}$ and $i+1$, $i+1$ of A^{-1}.

According to partitioned matrices the inverse of A is (cf. Goldberger, 1964, p. 27).

$$\begin{bmatrix} y'y & y'x \\ X'y & X'X \end{bmatrix}^{-1} = \begin{bmatrix} S & Q' \\ Q & P \end{bmatrix}$$

in which $S = M_k^{-1}$;

$M_k = y'y - y'X(X'X)^{-1}X'y$;

$Q = -(X'X)^{-1}X'yM_k^{-1}$;

$P = (X'X)^{-1} + (X'X)^{-1}X'yM_k^{-1}(y'X)(X'X)^{-1}$.

Also, according to the statistical formulas

$$M_k = (\mathrm{e}'\mathrm{e})_k \qquad Q = \frac{-b}{(\mathrm{e}'\mathrm{e})_k}$$

$$S = \frac{1}{(\mathrm{e}'\mathrm{e})_k} \qquad P = (X'X)^{-1} + \frac{bb'}{\mathrm{e}'\mathrm{e}_k}$$

so

$$A^{-1} = \frac{1}{(\mathrm{e}'\mathrm{e})_k}\begin{bmatrix} 1 & -b' \\ -b & \mathrm{e}'\mathrm{e}_k(X'X)^{-1} + bb' \end{bmatrix}. \tag{4.36}$$

From (4.35) and (4.36) it follows that

$$(\mathrm{e}'\mathrm{e})_{k-1} = (\mathrm{e}'\mathrm{e})_k \frac{A_{i+1,i+1}^{-1}}{(X'X)_{ii}^{-1}} = \frac{(\mathrm{e}'\mathrm{e})_k (X'X)_{ii}^{-1} + b_i^2}{(X'X)_{ii}^{-1}} =$$

$$= (\mathrm{e}'\mathrm{e})_k + \frac{b_i^2}{(X'X)_{ii}^{-1}}. \tag{4.37}$$

Since

$$(\mathrm{e}'\mathrm{e})_k = (T-k)\, s_k^2 \quad \text{and} \quad t_{b_i}^2 = \frac{b_i^2}{s_k^2 (X'X)_{ii}^{-1}}$$

it follows that

$$(T-k+1)\, s_{k-1}^2 = (T-k)\, s_k^2 + s_k^2 t_{b_i}^2$$

or

$$s_{k-1}^2 = \frac{T-k+t_{b_i}^2}{T-k+1} s_k^2. \tag{4.38}$$

Substitution of a value for $|t_{b_i}|$ smaller than, equal to or larger than 1 completes the proof.

One often uses instead of $|t_{b_i}|$ its reciprocal defined as the relative standard error ξ_i or b_i. The relationships in Lemma 3 are in that case

$$\begin{aligned} s_k^2 &< s_{k-1}^2 \quad \text{if and only if} \quad \xi_i < 1 \\ s_k^2 &= s_{k-1}^2 \quad \text{if and only if} \quad \xi_i = 1 \\ s_k^2 &> s_{k-1}^2 \quad \text{if and only if} \quad \xi_i > 1 . \end{aligned}$$

LEMMA 4

The value of q_A in model A is always larger than that of q_B in model B, in which

$$\begin{aligned} q_A &= X_\tau'(X'X)^{-1} X_\tau \\ q_B &= X_{1\tau}'(X_1'X_1)^{-1} X_{1\tau} \end{aligned}$$

Proof

Since X_1 is a submatrix of X, $X_1'X_1$ is a principal minor of $X'X$. Let this be the first one. Then assume $X'X=A$, $X_1'X_1=A_{11}$ and $X_\tau=z$. A and A_{11} are positive definite matrices of the order $k\times k$ respectively $(k-1)\times(k-1)$.

We can now write

$$\begin{aligned} A &= \begin{bmatrix} A_{11} & A_{12} \\ A_{21} & A_{22} \end{bmatrix} \\ q_A &= z'A^{-1}z \\ q_B &= z_1'A_{11}^{-1}z_1 . \end{aligned}$$

Transform z by means of $x=Pz$, in which

$$P = \begin{bmatrix} I & 0 \\ -A_{21}A_{11}^{-1} & I \end{bmatrix}$$

so that

$$x = \begin{bmatrix} x_1 \\ x_2 \end{bmatrix} = \begin{bmatrix} z_1 \\ -A_{21}A_{11}^{-1}z_1 + z_2 \end{bmatrix} .$$

It further holds that

$$\begin{aligned} z'A^{-1}z = (P^{-1}x)'\,A^{-1}(P^{-1}x) &= x'(P^{-1})'\,A^{-1}P^{-1}x \\ &= x'\,[PAP']^{-1}\,x . \end{aligned}$$

According to Anderson (1958, p. 343, Theorem 4)

$$PAP' = \begin{bmatrix} A_{11} & 0 \\ 0 & A_{11} - A_{12}A_{22}^{-1}A_{21} \end{bmatrix}.$$

So

$$z'A^{-1}z = z_1'A_{11}^{-1}z_1 + x_2'[A_{11} - A_{12}A_{22}^{-1}A_{21}]^{-1}x_2.$$

According to Anderson (1958, p. 337, Corollary 1 and 3) PAP' is positive definite and likewise $A_{11}-A_{12}A_{22}^{-1}A_{21}$.

So

$$z'A^{-1}z > z_1'A_{11}^{-1}z_1$$

or

$$q_A > q_B.$$

LEMMA 5

If $|t_{b_i}| \leqslant 1$ the $(1-\alpha)\%$ forecasting interval of model B is smaller than that of model A. This proposition formulates a condition sufficient but not necessary for the selction of B.

Proof

The $(1-\alpha)\%$ forecasting interval of the models A and B is proportional with $\det\theta\hat{\Omega}$ and so, by way of (3.39) and (3.41) in which $m=1$ it is also proportional with I_A and with I_B in which

$$I_A = F_\alpha(1, T-k)(1+q_A)S_A^2$$

$$I_B = F_\alpha(1, T-k+1)(1+q_B)S_B^2.$$

If $|t_{b_i}| \leqslant 1$, $s_B^2 \leqslant s_A^2$ according to Lemma 3.

Since, according to Lemma 4 $q_B < q_A$ and $F(1, h)$ is a declining function of h, so $F(1, h+1) < F(1, h)$, we have *a fortiori* $I_B < I_A$.

LEMMA 6

If model B is preferred over model A because of $|t_{b_i}| \leqslant 1$, the hypothesis $\beta_i = 0$ is also statistically tenable on the $(1-\alpha)\%$ level, provided $\alpha \leqslant 0.3$.

Proof

The hypothesis $\beta_i = 0$ cannot be rejected statistically, if for given α

$$|t_{b_i}| < t_\alpha.$$

If a model is chosen because $|t_{b_i}| \leqslant 1$, the specification of the model cannot be rejected if

$$t_\alpha \geqslant 1$$

so if

$$\int_{-t_\alpha}^{t_\alpha} \mathrm{d}t_{b_i} \geqslant \int_{-1}^{1} \mathrm{d}t_{b_i}$$

or if

$$\alpha = 1 - \int_{-t\alpha}^{t_\alpha} \mathrm{d}t_{b_i} \leqslant 1 - \int_{-1}^{1} \mathrm{d}t_{b_i} = 1 - t(h).$$

The value of $t(h)$ is a declining function of the number of degrees of freedom h. For $h \to \infty$ $t(h)$ tends to 0.68268 (see the table of the normal distribution). So with the actual percentage $\alpha = 0.05$ calling B a relevant model on account of $|t_{b_i}| \leqslant 1$ always implies that B is also statistically tenable with respect to the zerocoefficients. We can present the situation schematically as shown in Figure IV. 1.

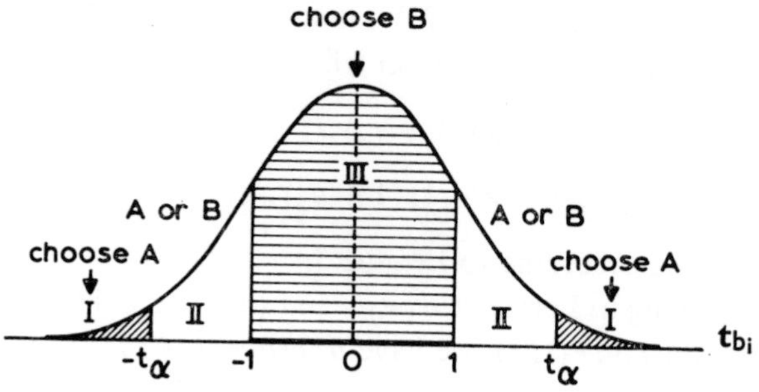

Fig. IV.1.

There are three area's:

I $\quad |t_{b_i}| \geqslant |t_\alpha|$ or $\xi_i \leqslant \dfrac{1}{|t_\alpha|}$.

The hypothesis $\beta_i = 0$ is rejected. Model B is not admitted.

II $\quad |t_\alpha| > |t_{b_i}| > 1 \quad \text{or} \quad 1 < \xi_i < \dfrac{1}{|t_\alpha|}.$

The hypothesis $\beta_i = 0$ and consequently also model B is admitted. The choice of A or B depends on the value of q.

III $\quad |t_{b_i}| \leqslant 1 \quad \text{or} \quad \xi_i \geqslant 1.$

Model B is admitted and has a smaller forecasting interval than model A, regardless of the value of q.

The value of q in both models depends on the situation of the exogeneous variables in the future. See Figure IV.2 for the case of a simple regression.

$$\mathbf{y}_t = \alpha + \beta X_t + \mathbf{u}_t .$$

The size of the forecasting interval is dependent on the situation of X in the forecasting period. The further away from $\bar{X}$, the mean in the reference period, the larger the forecasting interval.
However, if the regressionline is so unreliable that the relative standard error of the estimated regressioncoefficient becomes larger than 1, one would do better to take the model

$$\mathbf{y}_t = \alpha + \mathbf{u}_t$$

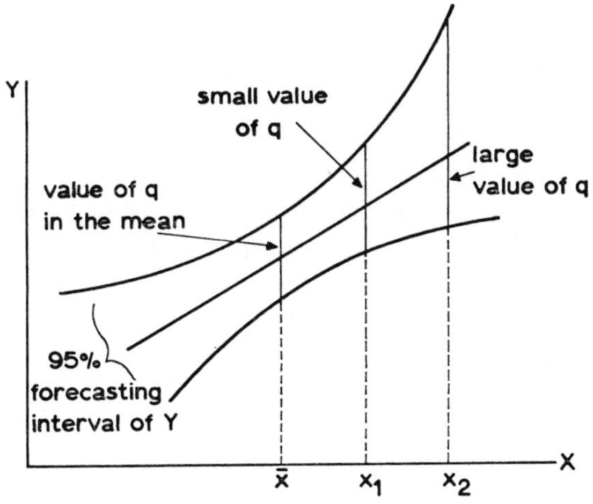

Fig. IV.2.

because, regardless of the position of X_t in the forecasting period, so even when $X_t = \bar{X}$, the interval of the latter model is smaller.

4.4.3. *More Equations*

When the model consists of more than 1 equation one can also derive an indicator that enables one to decide quickly whether elimination of a certain explanatory variable reduces the forecasting interval of the model, regardless of the values of the exogeneous variables in the forecasting period.

Assume

$$\mathbf{y}_t = \Pi X_t + \mathbf{v}_t \tag{4.39}$$

is a model with m equations, k explanatory variables and the usual characteristics for $\mathbf{v}_t$. Assume P is the matrix of the estimated regression-coefficients according to least squares and $P._i$ is the ith columh of P. So the latter contains the coefficients of X_i in the m equations.

Further assume $r = (X'X)_{ii}^{-1}$ is the ith diagonal element of $(X'X)^{-1}$. We can now prove the following lemma.

LEMMA 7

If

$$P'_i.(rE'E)^{-1} P._i \leqslant \left[1 + \frac{1}{T - k - m + 1}\right]^m - 1$$

from (4.39) a model can be obtained with a smaller interval by eliminating X_i from the model.

Proof

Assume $I(m, k)$ is the estimated interval of model (4.39) for the year τ. Assume $I(m, k-1; i)$ is the interval of the model that is obtained from (4.39) after the elimination of X_i, also measured in τ. According to Subsection 3.2.3.

$$I(m, k) > I(m, k - 1; i)$$

if

$$\frac{\det(\theta\hat{\Omega})_k}{\det(\theta\hat{\Omega})_{k-1}} > 1 \tag{4.40}$$

in which the indication i of the eliminated variable has been omitted for convenience's sake.

According to (3.39) we further have

$$\det(\theta\hat{\Omega})_k = \det[\theta_k(1+q_k)\,s_k] \tag{4.41}$$

while

$$s_k = \frac{(E'E)_k}{T-k} \tag{4.42}$$

in which E is the $T\times m$ matrix of the residuals of the regression of y on X_t.

Also according to (3.41)

$$\theta_k = \frac{(T-k)\,m}{T-k-m+1}\,F_\alpha(m, T-k-m+1)\,. \tag{4.43}$$

Substituting (4.43) and (4.42) in (4.41) we get

$$\det(\theta\hat{\Omega})_k = \left[\frac{m(1+q_k)\,F_\alpha(m, T-k-m+1)}{T-k-m+1}\right]^m \det E'E_k\,. \tag{4.44}$$

Substitution of (4.44) in (4.40) gives

$$\left[\frac{1+q_k}{1+q_{k-1}}\right]^m \left(\frac{F_k}{F_{k-1}}\right)^m \left[\frac{T-k-m+2}{T-k-m+1}\right]^m \frac{\det E'E_k}{\det E'E_{k-1}} > 1 \tag{4.45}$$

as the condition for $I(m, k) > I(m, k-1; i)$.

In this $F_k = F_\alpha(m, T-k-m+1)$. Since $q_k > q_{k-1}$, according to Lemma 4, and $F_k > F_{k-1}$ (4.45) has been satisfied, if

$$\left(\frac{T-k-m+2}{T-k-m+1}\right)^m \frac{\det E'E_k}{\det E'E_{k-1}} \geqslant 1\,. \tag{4.46}$$

For further analysis of (4.46) we form the $(m+k)\times(m+k)$ matrix

$$A^{-1} = \begin{bmatrix} Y'Y & Y'X \\ X'Y & X'X \end{bmatrix}^{-1} =$$

$$= \begin{bmatrix} (E'E)_k^{-1} & -(E'E)_k^{-1}P \\ -P'(E'E)_k^{-1} & P'(E'E)_k^{-1}P + (X'X)^{-1} \end{bmatrix}. \tag{4.47}$$

The latter equality follows again from the theory of partitioned matrices and the statistical formulas, e.g. (4.30). It is a generalisation of Formula (4.36) included in the proof of Lemma 3. With the help of Graybill (1961, p. 9) we write

$$\det A = \det X'X \det E'E_k$$

and analogous to (4.35)

$$\frac{\det E'E_{k-1}}{\det E'E_k} = \frac{\det A_{11}}{\det X_1'X_1} \frac{\det X'X}{\det A} \tag{4.48}$$

in which A_{11} and $X_1'X_1$ are the matrices obtained from respectively A and $X'X$ after the elimination of X_i, i.e. after the elimination of the $(m+i)$th respectively ith row and column of A and $X'X$. For (4.48) we can write, analogous to (4.37)

$$\frac{\det E'E_{k-1}}{\det E'E_k} = \frac{A^{-1}_{i+m,\,i+m}}{(X'X)^{-1}_{ii}} = \frac{r + P'_{i\cdot}(E'E)^{-1}_k P_{\cdot i}}{r}.$$

So

$$\frac{\det E'E_{k-1}}{\det E'E_k} = 1 + P'_{i\cdot}(rE'E)^{-1}_k P_{\cdot i}. \tag{4.49}$$

in which $r = (X'X)^{-1}_{ii}$ and $A^{-1}_{i+m,\,i+m}$ are the relevant elements of $(X'X)^{-1}$ and A^{-1}. Substitution of (4.49) in (4.46) gives as a sufficient condition for $I(m, k-1; i) < I(m, k)$

$$1 + P'_{i\cdot}(rE'E)^{-1}_k P_{\cdot i} \leqslant \left[1 + \frac{1}{T-k-m+1}\right]^m. \tag{4.50}$$

This completes the proof. An approximation can be found by

$$P'_{i\cdot}(rE'E)^{-1} P_{\cdot i} \leqslant \frac{m}{T-k-m+1}$$

in which only the first two terms of the expansion of the right-hand side of (4.50) have been taken into account. For $m=1$ Lemma 3 follows from Lemma 7. For diagonal $E'E$ the following relationship can be derived on the basis of Lemma 7.

$$\sum_{j=1}^{m} \mathbf{t}(\mathbf{P}_{ij}) < \frac{m(T-k)}{T-k-m+1}$$

in which $\mathbf{t}(\mathbf{P}_{ij})$ is the reciprocal of the relative standard error of the ith coefficient of the jth equation.

Summary

The course of the selection of the model with the optimal forecasting interval can now be summarized as follows:

(1) Form $\mathscr{T}$ (see Subsection 4.3.3).

(2) Construct from this the set $\mathscr{R}$ by eliminating non-relevant models from $\mathscr{T}$.

(3) Collect information about the value of the exogeneous variables in the forecasting period for the admitted relevant models.

(4) Calculate the forecasting intervals for the models of $\mathscr{R}$. The model with the smallest interval is chosen.

4.5. Some remarks on the use of lagged process variables

4.5.1

In this section a few remarks are made about the problems connected with the use of lagged process variables in the forecasting procedure.

We have reason to pay special attention to these variables as they give by their own the possibility of making forecasts for more than 1 period. However, in doing so, considerable problems arise. Those problems are such that we shall restrict ourselves to very simple models of 1 equation.

The problems are:

(1) The optimal forecasting *procedure* is no longer easy to determine.

(2) The calculation of the forecasting *interval* is, like the testing of the coefficients, only approximately valid.

(3) If one wishes to make a forecast more than 1 year ahead at least 1 of the 'explanatory' variables is also stochastic so that the forecasting procedure is no longer linear in the stochast added to the model.

Before we turn to the discussion of these problems it is desirable to indicate the place of the models discussed here, especially with respect to models with an autocorrelated disturbance. We start with the following model:

$$\mathbf{y}_t = \Pi X_t + \mathbf{v}_t \tag{4.51}$$
$$\mathbf{v}_t = \beta \mathbf{v}_{t-1} + \boldsymbol{\varepsilon}_t \tag{4.52}$$
$$\boldsymbol{\varepsilon}_t \cong N(0, \sigma^2) \quad \text{for every } t. \tag{4.53}$$

Π is a rowvector with length k. The other symbols are selfevident.

From the model follows:

$$\mathbf{y}_t = \beta \mathbf{y}_{t-1} + \Pi X_t + C X_{t-1} + \boldsymbol{\varepsilon}_t \tag{4.54}$$

in which

$$C = \Pi \beta . \tag{4.55}$$

Apart from this one can also consider the model that consists of (4.54) together with (4.53) but without the restriction (4.55). In the latter case one speaks of a stochastic dynamic model without autocorrelation. With (4.55) one speaks of a stochastic (static) model with autocorrelation. These models do not only differ in (4.55), for that matter. In case of a model with autocorrelation one starts from $|\beta|<1$. In a dynamic model β can also be larger than 1.

Analogous to the previous sections we shall here only discuss models without restrictions on the coefficients. So only models without autocorrelation come up for discussion. As a matter of fact, the dynamic model coincides with the model with autocorrelation, if $\Pi = C = 0$ and $\beta \leqslant 1$. In that case we get for (4.54)

$$\mathbf{y}_t = \beta \mathbf{y}_{t-1} + \boldsymbol{\varepsilon}_t . \tag{4.56}$$

Together with (4.53), (4.56) forms the model to which we restrict ourselves to begin with.

4.5.2

First we shall discuss the problem of the optimal forecasting procedure. Assume that we determine the forecasting procedure as if $\mathbf{y}_{t-1}$ were an exogeneous variable instead of a lagged endogeneous variable. This results in

$$\hat{\mathbf{y}}_t = \hat{\boldsymbol{\beta}}\, \mathbf{y}_{t-1} \tag{4.57}$$

with $\hat{\boldsymbol{\beta}}$ as least squares estimator of β. This forecasting procedure need not be optimal neither in form nor in the way in which β has been estimated. Qua form one might e.g. consider to draw y_{t-2}, y_{t-3} etc. into the procedure. We shall revert to this. For the time being we assume that the form of the forecasting procedure is given and that only the coefficients must yet be determined. If $|\beta|<1$ according to Mann and Wald (1943)

$\hat{\boldsymbol{\beta}}$ is a consistent estimator of β and asymptotically normal distributed. According to Rubin (1950) $\hat{\boldsymbol{\beta}}$ is also a consistent estimator if $|\beta|>1$. Therefore, for large samples and given the form (4.57) may be considered to be approximately optimal. For small samples this is not necessarily true. But, according to Malinvaud, (1964, p. 463) $\hat{\mathbf{y}}_t$ from (4.57) is an unbiased predictor in that case. This is confirmed by simulations of Malinvaud (1961) and Orcutt and Winokur (1969). Malinvaud starts in his simulation from

$$\mathbf{y}_t = 0.6\mathbf{y}_{t-1} + 0.4x_t + \boldsymbol{\varepsilon}_t \tag{4.58}$$

and (4.53) with given $\sigma=6$, together with 2 other distributions for $\boldsymbol{\varepsilon}_t$.
His conclusion is that

> ... the results obtained on the samples examined suggest that the formulas associated with the least squares method are approximately valid for the treatment of model (4.58) when the disturbances are not autocorrelated.

Orcutt and Winokur start from (4.56) with respectively $\beta=0$, 0.5 and 0.9 yet they add an $\hat{\alpha}$ to (4.57). Their conclusion is "Standard least squares seems to be nearly optimal in small samples and has a smaller prediction variance than predictions using a corrected least squares estimate of β". In the corrected forecasting procedures discussed by the authors the estimate $\hat{\beta}$ in (4.57) has been replaced by an unbiased estimate of β, based on studies by Mariott and Pope (1954) and Quenoille (1949). The latter study did not offer any possibilities to improve the forecasting procedure. The former, in which

$$\beta^* = \frac{T}{T-3}\hat{\boldsymbol{\beta}} + \frac{T}{T-3}$$

takes the place of $\hat{\beta}$ in (4.57) turned out to give an unbiased estimate of $E\hat{\mathbf{y}}_t$ with a smaller mean square prediction error than (4.57), but only for higher values of β – i.e. if $T=20$ the forecasting procedure is only unbiased when roughly $|\beta|> 0.7$.

A curious thing here is the fact that Orcutt and Winokur start from model (4.56), so without a constant, yet have not tried

$$\beta^{**} = \frac{T}{T-2}\hat{\beta} \quad \text{and} \quad \alpha^{**} = 0$$

in their forecasting procedure.

For, if (4.56) does not contain a constant

$$E\hat{\boldsymbol{\beta}} = \frac{T-2}{T}\beta + 0(T^{-1})$$

according to Hurwicz (1950) or Malinvaud (1954, p. 460.) Whatever the case may be, it can be stated on the ground of the simulations mentioned that as soon as the form of (4.57) is given, the forecasting with the least squares estimates is the best known approximation of the optimal forecasting procedure, corresponding to (4.56), provided the value of β is not too close to 1. The latter is usually the case with macro-economic time series based on yearly figures. One normally finds values for $\hat{\beta}$ like 0.4 to 0.5.

4.5.3

Apart from the fact that (4.57) is approximately optimal, the simulation studies mentioned show that for given y_{-1} the usual formulas to calculate the forecasting interval are valid.

So we get as the estimate of var $\mathbf{e}_t$

$$(1 + y_{t-1}^2)\, s_\varepsilon^2 \tag{4.59}$$

in which

$$s_\varepsilon^2 = \frac{\sum_{i=2}^{T} \hat{\boldsymbol{\varepsilon}}_i^2}{T-2} \tag{4.60}$$

and $\boldsymbol{\varepsilon}_i$ the residual of the year i in the regression of y_t on y_{t-1} without a constant and T observations. Moreover, the estimation of var$\hat{\boldsymbol{\beta}}$ is approximately

$$\frac{s_\varepsilon^2}{\sum_{t=2}^{T} y_{t-1}^2}. \tag{4.61}$$

As a matter of fact, in our calculations in Chapter V the results with (4.61) appeared to differ only slightly from calculations made with the help of an approximating formula of the order T^{-1} that can be taken from Shenton and Johnson (1965) namely

$$\operatorname{var} \hat{\boldsymbol{\beta}} = \frac{(1-\beta^2)}{T-1} - \frac{(1-14\beta^2)}{(T-1)^2} \tag{4.62}$$

if in the right-hand side the estimate $\tilde{\boldsymbol{\beta}}$ is substituted for β. To be true, for smaller values of β and larger values of T (4.62) leads to

$$\operatorname{var} \hat{\boldsymbol{\beta}} \approx \frac{1-\beta^2}{T-1} \tag{4.63}$$

which can already be found with Malinvaud (1964, p. 460). The curious thing about (4.62) and (4.63) is the fact that they do not contain the parameter σ. Moreover, it appears from (4.61) that σ occurs both in the numerator and in the denominator, so that the quotient is approximately independent of σ. Of course (4.62) and (4.63) are only approximations. If $\sigma \to 0$ one does not get a correct result when using these formulas, but one does if (4.61) is used.

Also the testing of the hypothesis $\beta = 0$ can take place approximately according to the usual formulas. For, according to Orcutt and Winokur (1969) the magnitude $\hat{\boldsymbol{\beta}}/\mathbf{s}_\beta$ follows a t-distribution very closely, also in small samples.

It is interesting to examine on the basis of the approximating formulas whether model (4.56) together with (4.53) is preferred over

$$\mathbf{y}_t = \boldsymbol{\varepsilon}_t \cong N(0, \sigma) \quad \text{for every } t. \tag{4.64}$$

We approximate $\hat{\boldsymbol{\beta}}/\mathbf{s}_\beta$ or its square with the help of (4.63) by

$$\frac{(T-1)\,\hat{\boldsymbol{\beta}}^2}{1-\hat{\boldsymbol{\beta}}^2}.$$

This magnitude has approximately an $F(1, T-2)$ distribution. Model (4.64) is not admitted as far as the coefficients are concerned if

$$\frac{(T-1)\,\hat{\beta}^2}{1-\hat{\beta}^2} > F_\alpha(1, T-2)$$

or if

$$\hat{\beta}^2 > \frac{F_\alpha(1, T-2)}{T-1+F_\alpha(1, T-2)}.$$

If the latter is true, (4.56) together with (4.53) is chosen. On the other hand, model (4.64) is admitted and relevant if

$$\frac{(T-1)\,\hat{\beta}^2}{1-\hat{\beta}^2} < 1$$

or if

$$\beta^2 < \frac{1}{T}.$$

For $T=20$ and $\alpha=0.05$ this means that it is not to the point to include $\mathbf{y}_{t-1}$ in the specification if $|\hat{\beta}| < 0.22$[20] but it is required if $|\hat{\beta}| > 0.43$. These figures link up well with the results obtained by Rao and Griliches (1969) in a somewhat different connection. Based on a simulation of samples of 20 random drawings, generated by the model

$$\mathbf{y}_t = \beta \mathbf{y}_{t-1} + \\ + \Pi_1 (X_{1t} - \beta X_{1,t-1}) + \cdots + \Pi_k (X_{kt} - \beta X_{k,t-1}) + \boldsymbol{\varepsilon}_t$$

with (4.53), they reach the conclusion that, especially if $|\beta| > 0.3$ it is more advantageous to estimate β than to assume it is zero, because with the use of an efficient estimation method[21] the stochasticity of the estimate cancels out against the sophistication of the method.

Finally, it should be pointed out that the well-known tests on autocorrelation are all based on relations in which only exogeneous variables occur. Recently Durbin (1970) proposed a test for relationships in which also lagged exogeneous variables occur. The teststatistic **h** derived by him is a transformation of the Durbin-Watson statistic **d** and can only be used with large samples. Durbin does not give any applications. It is not clear yet to what extent the use of **d** will lead to incorrect conclusions when the explanatory variables are lagged endogeneous variables as opposed to exogeneous ones. In Chapter V we have used the statistic **d** for testing on autocorrelation, also in case of lagged endogeneous variables.

4.5.4

The simulations of Orcutt and Cochrane (1949) and Malinvaud (1961) show that the conclusions drawn with respect to model (4.56) change if the assumption $E\boldsymbol{\varepsilon}\boldsymbol{\varepsilon}' = \sigma^2 I$ is replaced by a hypothesis of existing autocorrelation, in other words if (4.56) is replaced by

$$\mathbf{y}_t = (\beta + \rho)\,\mathbf{y}_{t-1} - \beta\rho\mathbf{y}_{t-2} + \boldsymbol{\varepsilon}_t \tag{4.65}$$

with the same characteristics for $\boldsymbol{\varepsilon}_t$. However, an evaluation of this model set against a model without restrictions on the coefficients is no more known than in the case of (4.54) with or without $C=0$. So we shall neglect (4.65) and only admit

$$\mathbf{y}_t = \beta_1\mathbf{y}_{t-1} + \beta_2\mathbf{y}_{t-2} + \boldsymbol{\varepsilon}_t \tag{4.66}$$

with (4.53) and without restrictions on β_i. Estimation procedures for (4.66) have been examined to a lesser extent then those for (4.56). However one usually takes the line that least squares give a good approximation, also in this case.[22] For large samples and difference equations the moduli of the roots of which are smaller than 1 the justification can be based on Mann and Wald (1943). However, for small samples the importance is not quite clear yet. We shall not go into this matter any further and assume in our calculations that the least squares give a good approximation in determining the optimal forecasting procedure and also that the usual formulas to calculate the forecasting interval are valid.

A more general model is

$$\mathbf{y}_t = \beta_1\mathbf{y}_{t-1} + \beta_2\mathbf{y}_{t-2} + \cdots + \beta_N\mathbf{y}_{t-N} + \boldsymbol{\varepsilon}_t \tag{4.67}$$

with (4.53).

In order to determine the optimal forecasting procedure, given the form one may again apply least squares as an approximation. The determination of the largest lag that is still useful depends on the size of the forecasting interval. In this it is possible to have $\beta_j=0$ for $j<N$, whereas $\beta_N \neq 0$. This is not the case with other methods that make a choice between (4.66) and (4.67) with $N>2$. See e.g. Malinvaud (1964, p. 488)

4.5.5

As it has been said before, the forecasting procedure need not always have the same form as the model.

$$\mathbf{y}_t = \delta_1\mathbf{y}_{t-1} + \delta_2\mathbf{y}_{t-2} + \cdots + \delta_N\mathbf{y}_{t-N} \tag{4.68}$$

with e.g.

$$\delta_i = 1/N \tag{4.69}$$

can also be considered a forecasting procedure belonging to model (4.56) with (4.53).

In that case there is no estimation problem left.[23] The forecasting procedure is the moving average with period N, namely

$$\hat{\mathbf{y}}_t = 1/N \sum_{i=1}^{N} \mathbf{y}_{t-i}. \tag{4.70}$$

This brings us to the method of the 'controllers'. They restrict themselves to forecasting procedures such as (4.68) together with (4.69) or to (4.68) with another rule to determine δ_i. The controllers do not determine the coefficients of (4.68) by means of a model. As a matter of fact, they do not have a uniform criterion either about the question how large N should be, or about the size of δ_i. According to van Winkel (1970, p. 50) the N is determined as a compromise between the desired smoothing and the speed with which one wishes to point out the changes in the structure. The simplest method is (4.70). In this method N is chosen freely. A second possibility is that of the 'proportional correction', in which (4.68) is used together with

$$\delta_i = \alpha(1-\alpha)^{i-1} \tag{4.71}$$

for given α. In this method the N in (4.68) is fixed by the desired numerical precision. It can be demonstrated with the help of van Winkel (1970, p. 64) that with respect to the model

$$\mathbf{y}_t = \gamma + \boldsymbol{\varepsilon}_t \tag{4.72}$$

$$E\boldsymbol{\varepsilon}_t = 0 \tag{4.73}$$

$$E\boldsymbol{\varepsilon}_t\boldsymbol{\varepsilon}_{t'} = \begin{cases} \sigma^2 & \text{for} \quad t = t' \\ 0 & \text{for} \quad t \neq t'. \end{cases} \tag{4.74}$$

(4.71) is preferable to (4.70) if

$$\alpha < \frac{2}{N+1} \tag{4.75}$$

This implies that the mean of a sample of T-values does not give the optimal forecasting interval of the above model, since (4.68), (4.71) and (4.75) lead to a better forecasting procedure. In specifying the procedure the only parameter α must be chosen in the interval

$$0 < \alpha < \frac{2}{T+1}.$$

Van Winkel also introduces models with noise. This means in fact that (4.72) is replaced by (4.56) after a constant has been added, so by

$$\mathbf{y}_t = \beta \mathbf{y}_{t-1} + \gamma + \boldsymbol{\varepsilon}_t \qquad |\beta| < 1 \tag{4.76}$$

in which β is the autocorrelation coefficient. The controllers do not estimate the parameters explicitly, so neither β, as a result of which the estimation problems previously mentioned do not occur. The latter implies that neither δ_i must be chosen after one has seen the observations, nor a δ_i can be looked for, which is optimal with respect to β, without corrupting the formulas used by the controllers. It is interesting to notice that van Winkel investigates which value of α in (4.71) is optimal with respect to model (4.76) with (4.73) and (4.74). He arrives at the conclusion that for $-1 < \beta \leqslant \frac{1}{3}$ the optimal value of α is 0. It is not quite clear what the forecasting procedure is in that case, for, with the method of proportional corrections, we have the condition $1 > \alpha > 0$. We interpret van Winkel's optimality rule in such a way that for $-1 \leqslant \beta < \frac{1}{3}$ $\hat{y}_t = 0$[24] becomes the best choice. In Cox's method (1961), autocorrelation is explicitly taken into account. His forecasting procedure is:

$$\hat{\mathbf{y}}_t = \beta \mathbf{y}_{t-1} + (1 - \beta)\, \hat{\mathbf{y}}_t^* \tag{4.77}$$

in which $\hat{\mathbf{y}}_t^*$ is the forecast according to proportional correction, so (4.68) after substitution of (4.71) for given α and N. According to van Winkel (1970, p. 74), if $\delta = 1$, or $\alpha = 0$, (4.77) is with respect to (4.76) preferable to $\hat{\mathbf{y}}_t = \hat{\mathbf{y}}_t^*$, regardless of the value of β. The variance of the forecasting error of (4.77) is then smaller than that of $\hat{\mathbf{y}}_t^*$.

However, for $\alpha = 0$, (4.77) becomes

$$\hat{\mathbf{y}}_t = \beta \mathbf{y}_{t-1}\,. \tag{4.78}$$

This means that for $-1 < \beta < \frac{1}{3}$, so in which $\alpha = 0$ is optimal, (4.78) is preferable to $\hat{\mathbf{y}}_t = 0$, which in turn is better than a common moving average.

However, this result is affected if β must be estimated. The broad outlines we indicated in Subsection 4.5.3 then point to another choice, namely $\hat{\mathbf{y}}_t = 0$, if $|\hat{\beta}| < 0.23$.

4.5.6

Assume we use $\hat{y}_t = \hat{\beta} y_{t-1}$ as a procedure for forecasts one year ahead, because in that procedure the forecasting error has an expectation 0 and the variance of the forecasting error is small. The procedure mentioned cannot be used for more than one year, as the explanatory variable is not known then. However, with help of model (4.56) we can transform the forecasting formula back to the last known value, so that we get the following system of equations:

$$\mathbf{y}_{t+\lambda} = \beta^{\lambda+1} y_{t-1} + [\boldsymbol{\varepsilon}_{t+\lambda} + \beta \boldsymbol{\varepsilon}_{t+\lambda-1} + \cdots + \beta^{\lambda} \boldsymbol{\varepsilon}_t] \tag{4.79}$$

$$\lambda = 1, 2, \ldots, \tau .$$

If we only need a forecast for the year $t+\tau$, we merely select the equation with $t=\tau$, so

$$\mathbf{y}_{t+\tau} = \gamma \mathbf{y}_{t-1} + \mathbf{v}_t \tag{4.80}$$

with

$$\gamma = \beta^{\tau+1} \tag{4.81}$$

$$\mathbf{v}_t = \boldsymbol{\varepsilon}_{t+\tau} + \beta \boldsymbol{\varepsilon}_{t+\tau-1} + \cdots + \beta^{\tau} \boldsymbol{\varepsilon}_t . \tag{4.82}$$

The restriction to a model with one equation takes place with reference to Lemma 2. A strict proof is not valid here, for Lemma 2 relates merely to models with only exogeneous variables as explanators.

Instead of model (4.80) with (4.53) and the restrictions (4.81) and (4.82) one can also choose a model without restrictions namely (4.80) with $\mathbf{v}_t \cong N(0, \sigma^2)$. The forecasting procedure is then

$$y_{t+\tau} = \hat{\gamma} y_{t-1} \tag{4.83}$$

with $\hat{\gamma}$ the least squares estimate of $y_{t+\tau}$ on y_{t-1}. It is not clear to what extent the latter combination of model and forecasting procedure is preferable to the model comprised in (4.80), (4.81) (4.82) and (4.53) in combination with the procedure[25]

$$\hat{y}_{t+\tau} = \hat{\beta}^{\tau+1} y_{t-1} . \tag{4.84}$$

Although ee have continually disregarded the problem of the restrictions, we allow ourselves here a few remarks on the model with restictions to stress the problem.

(4.84) in combination with the underlying model has the following forecasting error

$$\mathbf{e}_{t+\tau} = \mathbf{y}_{t+\tau} - \hat{\mathbf{y}}_{t+\tau} = y_{t-1}\,[\beta^{\tau+1} - \hat{\boldsymbol{\beta}}^{\tau+1}] + \mathbf{v}_t . \tag{4.85}$$

So

$$\operatorname{var}\mathbf{e}_{t+\tau} = y_{t-1}^2 \operatorname{var}\hat{\boldsymbol{\beta}}^{\tau+1} + \operatorname{var}\mathbf{v}_t \tag{4.86}$$

or, by (4.82)

$$\operatorname{var}\mathbf{e}_{t+\tau} = y_{t-1}^2 \operatorname{var}\hat{\boldsymbol{\beta}}^{\tau+1} + [1 + \beta + \cdots + \beta^{2\tau}]\,\sigma^2 . \tag{4.87}$$

According to Cramér (1946, p. 353–354) the following holds approximately

$$\operatorname{var}\phi(\mathbf{u},\mathbf{v}) = \left(\frac{\partial\mu}{\partial\mathbf{u}}\right)^2 \operatorname{var}\mathbf{u} + \left(\frac{\partial\mu}{\partial\mathbf{v}}\right)^2 \operatorname{var}\mathbf{v} + \\ + 2\left(\frac{\partial\mu}{\partial\mathbf{u}}\right)\left(\frac{\partial\mu}{\partial\mathbf{v}}\right)\operatorname{cov}(\mathbf{u}.\,\mathbf{v}) .$$

Applied to (4.87) this gives

$$\operatorname{var}\mathbf{e}_{t+\tau} = y_{t-1}^2\,[(\tau+1)\,\hat{\boldsymbol{\beta}}^{\tau}]^2 \operatorname{var}\hat{\boldsymbol{\beta}} + \sigma^2\,[1 + \beta^2 + \cdots + \beta^{2\tau}]. \tag{4.88}$$

Replacement of β by $\hat{\beta}$ and of σ^2 by s^2 gives an estimation formula for $\operatorname{var}\mathbf{e}_{t+\tau}$. Since we further have approximately

$$\operatorname{var}\hat{\boldsymbol{\beta}} = \frac{s^2}{\sum y_{t-1}^2} \quad \text{and} \quad q = \frac{y_{t-1}^2}{\sum y_{t-1}^2}$$

we can also write for the estimation of $\operatorname{var}\mathbf{e}_{t+\tau}$

$$\widehat{\operatorname{var}\mathbf{e}_{t+\tau}} = qs^2(1+\tau)^2\,\hat{\beta}^{2\tau} + \frac{1-\hat{\beta}^{2\tau+2}}{1-\hat{\beta}^2}\,s^2 . \tag{4.89}$$

If two years must be predicted at the same time, one needs two of the equations of (4.79) instead of one, e.g. for $\lambda = 1.2$ we get

$$\begin{aligned} \mathbf{y}_t &= \beta y_{t-1} + \boldsymbol{\varepsilon}_t \\ \mathbf{y}_{t+1} &= \beta^2 y_{t-1} + \beta\boldsymbol{\varepsilon}_t + \boldsymbol{\varepsilon}_{t+1} . \end{aligned} \tag{4.90}$$

Assume we choose

$$\begin{aligned} \hat{\mathbf{y}}_t &= \tilde{\boldsymbol{\beta}} y_{t-1} \\ \hat{\mathbf{y}}_{t+1} &= \tilde{\boldsymbol{\beta}}^2 y_{t-1} \end{aligned} \tag{4.91}$$

as forecasting procedure, in which $\tilde{\boldsymbol{\beta}}$ is an unbiased estimator of β, so

$$E\hat{\mathbf{y}}_t = \beta y_{t-1} \quad \text{and} \quad \operatorname{var} \hat{\mathbf{y}}_t = \sigma^2 .$$

However, we now also have

$$E\hat{\mathbf{y}}_{t+1} = y_{t-1} E\tilde{\boldsymbol{\beta}}^2 = y_{t-1} [\operatorname{var} \tilde{\beta} + \beta^2]$$

and the latter is only equal to $\beta^2 y_{t-1}$, if $\operatorname{var} \tilde{\beta} = 0$. So no unbiased estimator $\tilde{\beta}$ of β can be found which in (4.91) gives an expected forecasting error of zero both in the first and in the second year.[26]

So with forecasts for more than one year ahead either the requirement $E\mathbf{e}_{t+\lambda} = 0$ for all λ must be dropped, or one must look for a procedure with a form different from (4.91).

As it is, in this kind of models the variances of the autocorrelation coefficient can usually be neglected with respect to those of the explanatory variable. This is apparent from the simulations by Malinvaud (1961) and Orcutt and Winokur (1969). So, as an approximation of (4.89) we usually find that

$$\widehat{\operatorname{var} \mathbf{e}_{t+\tau}} \approx \frac{1 - \beta^{2\tau+2}}{1 - \beta^2} s^2 \qquad (4.92)$$

is satisfactory. (4.92) has been obtained through (4.88) by substitution of $\operatorname{var} \hat{\boldsymbol{\beta}} \approx 0$[27]. This implies at the same time that Cox's method, mentioned before, can also be used for estimated β without taking the variance of $\hat{\boldsymbol{\beta}}$ into account.

As the variance of $\mathbf{e}_{t+\tau}$ increases with increasing β an overestimation β implies also an overestimation of $\operatorname{var} \mathbf{e}_{t+\tau}$[28]. To compensate for the neglect of $\operatorname{var} \hat{\boldsymbol{\beta}}$ in the formula for $\operatorname{var} \mathbf{e}_{t+\tau}$ one might increase $\hat{\beta}$ somewhat for the calculation of the forecasting interval. So in the calculation of s^2 one must take this overestimation into account. I.e. we then define

$$s^{*2} = \frac{\sum [y_t - (1 + \lambda) \hat{\beta} y_{t-1}]^2}{T - 1}$$

in which $\hat{\beta}$ is the least squares estimate of β and λ a small positive number. In (4.92) $\hat{\beta}$ is then also replaced by $(1 + \lambda)\hat{\beta}$. In Chapter V an example of this will be given.

NOTES TO CHAPTER IV

1 See also Hooper and Zellner (1961).

2 For $m=1$ we get $\theta=F(1, T-k)$ see (3.41).

3 The problem of the significance of R^2 (see Koerts and Abrahamse (1969)) is not important here, because a choice must also be made when $R_1{}^2$ does not differ significantly from $R_2{}^2$.

4 See e.g. Christ (1966, p. 509). $\bar{R}^2$ must be distinguished from the $\hat{R}^2$ that is proposed by Barten (1962), namely

$$\hat{R}^2 = R^2 - (1/T)(1-R^2)\,[k-(1-R^2)(1+2R^2)]$$

5 See e.g. 10th Flemish Congress (1971, p. 53 ff.).

6 Including this factor q in the choice of the model will often result in linear trends being preferred in linear models to trends of a higher order. For, with the latter the deviation between the new value of the exogeneous variables and the average value in the past will be larger. So, in order to be chosen in spite of this, a trend of a higher degree must give an adjustment that is significantly better.

7 See (3.69).

8 Just to mention a few Theil (1965, Chapter 2), Stekler (1968), van den Beld (1965).

9 See Cramer (1969, p. 82).

10 See (3.23).

11 See Section 2.4.

12 In fact there are 3 tests, because (4.23) has two different aspects: (4.23a) and (4.23b).

13 See e.g. Glejser (1969), Goldfeld and Quandt (1965) or Theil (1971 p. 214 ff.).

14 Short for: testing on the absence of autocorrelation and testing on homoskedasticity.

15 In the calculations in Chapter V the so-called relative standard error $\xi_i = S_{b_i}/b_i$ is compared with the reciprocal values of the t-table in order to link up with certain standard computer programs.

16 See Subsection 3.3.3.

17 Here Y is defined as a $T\times m$ matrix instead of an $m\times T$ matrix as we did previously.

18 $\hat{\Sigma}$ is not an unbiased estimator of Σ in (4.23)! An unbiased estimator is

$$S=\frac{T}{T-K}\hat{\Sigma}_k$$

19 See (4.49).

20 Or $|\beta^{**}|<0.25$.

21 Rao and Griliches mention Durbin's (1960) 2-step regression method as being the most efficient one. With this method first β is estimated from a regression of y_t on $y_{t-1}, X_{t,1}, X_{t-1,1}, \ldots X_{t,k}$, and $X_{t,k-1}$ and afterwards the values of Π_i are estimated from a regression of $(y_t-\bar{\beta}y_{t-1})$ on $(X_{t,1}-\bar{\beta}X_{t-1,1})\ldots(X_{t,k}-\bar{\beta}X_{t-1,k})$ in which $\bar{\beta}$ is the first round estimator of β.

22 See e.g. Malinvaud (1961, p. 27).

23 Except in some instances the N.

24 $\delta_i=0$ in (4.68) for $i=1,2,\ldots,N$ gives $\hat{y}_t=0$. However, as van Winkel pointed out to me lately, $\hat{y}_t=y_{t-1}$ for $\alpha=0$ would be more conform the additional requirement $\Sigma\delta_i=1$.

[25] Den Butter (1972) has recently compared both methods mentioned for $\tau = 2$ in a number of simulations starting from $\mathbf{y}_t = \alpha + \beta \mathbf{y}_{t-1} + \mathbf{u}_t$ with several values of α and β. On the basis of the results of all simulations combined (4.84) appeared to be significantly superior to (4.83).

[26] See den Butter (1972).

[27] Or by way of (4.89) with $q \approx 0$.

[28] See (4.88). In case of large τ and $\hat{\boldsymbol{\beta}} < 1$ the first term can be neglected.

CHAPTER V

EXAMPLES

5.1. Introduction

In this chapter examples are given of some aspects of the previous theoretical considerations but on a minor scale. The applications concern the export surplus of the Netherlands $\mathbf{Q}_t$ and the Gross National Product $\mathbf{Y}_t$.

In Section 5.2 our aim is the simultaneous forecast of $\mathbf{Q}_t$ for 1966 and 1967 on the basis of the reference period 1948–1965 inc. In Section 5.3 the forecast of $\mathbf{Q}_t$ for 1966 only. In Section 5.4 the forecast of $\mathbf{Y}_t$ for 1966 and in the last Section 5.5 the simultaneous forecast of $\mathbf{Y}_t$ and $\mathbf{Q}_t$ for 1966, always on the basis of the same reference period.

The examples are merely meant as illustrations of certain aspects of the suggested procedure. Our startingpoint was not a (truncated) maximum specification. It seemed more useful to demonstrate the problems by way of small groups of models. The models have been indicated as follows

$$QY\,[Q_{-1}\;Y_{-1}\;c].$$

This means that Q and Y are the endogeneous variables in which Q is the first one and Y the second one. Q_{-1}, Y_{-1} and a constant are the explanatory variables in that order.

In Section 5.2 only 1 group of models is discussed, namely those models that can be derived from

$$S(4) = Q\,[t^3\;\;t^2\;\;t\;\;c].$$

This implies there are $2^4 - 1 = 15$ models[1]. In Section 5.3 one finds apart from the former group still four other groups, together comprising 18 models. A survey of the 33 models that are considered available in the forecast of Q_t in 1966 can be found in Table V.5[2]. The timeseries used are presented in Table V.1. Apart from the 33 models that generate unconditional forecasts of Q_t, 2 models are discussed with which only conditional forecasts can be made. Inside each group of models the test- and selection procedure takes place, as described in Chapter IV, that is tests on zerocoefficients and on autocorrelation are only carried out inside the group. Moreover, simultaneous tests on more than 1 zerocoefficient were omitted for the larger part.

In Section 5.4, 3 groups have been introduced for the forecast of $\mathbf{Y}_t$, together comprising 25 models. This Section 5.4 was inserted exclusively as a step towards the simultaneous forecast of $\mathbf{Y}_t$ and $\mathbf{Q}_t$ in Section 5.5. In the latter section only 1 group of 7 models is discussed.

It must be stressed here that these examples are of hardly any significance as a real application of the suggested forecasting procedure. For this purpose the set-up is too fragmentary, the information used too meagre and the set of models too small. With an actual application one shall have to start from a much larger number of explanatory variables.

Although the given examples are only meant as illustrations we have not been able to resist the temptation to investigate how the optimal forecasting procedure for the forecast of the export surplus based on the 33 models presented in Section 3.3 would have performed in the sixties. It will not be surprising that this optimal forecasting procedure appears to possess so wide an interval that all values of the sixties are caught. Yet, it is surprising indeed, that in general this procedure would have lead to smaller forecasting errors than those that are connected with the forecasts published by the Central Planning Bureau. Of course, this does not imply that the methods used there should be replaced completely. For the models of the Central Planning Bureau are not only constructed with the aim of giving forecasts, but also to give a diagnosis of the recent developments and to provide a basis for future government policies.

5.2. The Forecast of the Export Surplus for Two Years

5.2.1. *The General Set-up*

Let us assume that we have to give a prediction of the export surplus[3] of the Netherlands for 1966 and 1967. We have the data on 1948–1965 inc. at our disposal (see Table V.1)[4].

For the prediction we only consider the group of 15 models that can be derived from $Q[t^3\ t^2\ t\ c]$. The discussion takes place by means of Table V.2. It should be emphasized that all models are linear with a normally distributed disturbance. Since only $\mathbf{Q}_t$ must be forecasted, the models consist of only 1 equation, according to Lemma 2. The variables

TABLE V.1

Some basic data for the Netherlands (1948–1965) (billions of guilders)

Year	Export surplus	Gross National product	Export	Import	Unemploy-ment[a]	World trade[b]
	Q_t	Y_t	B_t	M_t	$\tilde{w}_t$	b_e
1948	−1.52	15.06	4.60	6.12	2.6	
9	−0.41	17.03	6.08	6.49	2.3	9.0
1950	−1.22	18.90	8.15	9.37	2.8	19.3
1	−0.31	21.65	10.82	11.13	3.2	10.3
2	1.72	22.69	11.85	10.13	4.8	2.1
3	1.33	24.20	12.12	10.79	3.7	3.3
4	0.22	27.00	13.32	13.10	2.5	9.6
1955	0.78	30.28	15.03	14.25	1.7	12.3
6	−0.71	32.57	16.21	16.92	1.3	7.4
7	−0.54	35.36	17.94	18.48	1.6	6.8
8	1.56	35.93	18.10	16.54	3.1	1.4
9	1.84	38.44	20.07	18.23	2.4	9.6
1960	1.27	42.73	22.59	21.23	1.5	14.1
1	0.70	45.29	22.96	22.26	1.1	5.1
2	0.63	48.51	24.30	23.67	1.0	8.9
3	0.29	52.86	26.48	26.19	1.0	8.2
4	−0.55	62.16	30.23	30.78	0.9	10.7
1965[c]	0.25	68.99	33.36	33.11	1.0	9.2

Source: CEP (1968) p. 180–181: 1950–1965 inc. Information CPB: 1948 and 1949.

[a] As a percentage of the labour force.
[b] Increase of world demand, in percentages, weighed according to the relative shares of Dutch export markets.
[c] The figure for 1965 proved, on the basis of later data, to be not yet definite, CEP (1971) gives the following figures:

0.28	69.37	33.24	32.96	1.0	9.4

t^3, t^2, t and c all have the value 1 in 1948 and respectively 8, 4, 2, and 1 in 1949, etc.

Since we begin the analysis with the specification $S(4; t^3\ t^2\ t\ c)$, the model is not tested on zerocoefficients, but only on autocorrelation. The computed Durbin-Watson statistic d appears to have the value 1.51 which is larger than the critical value d_L at the 95% level.[5] So model $Q\,[t^3\ t^2\ t\ c]$ is admitted.

All specifications $S(3)$ that arise from $S(4)$ through elimination of one of the variables appear to be admitted as well. Indeed, for each of them $d > d_L$ and, moreover, in $S(4)$, $\xi_i > \xi_\alpha$ for all i.

It appears that on the basis of model $Q[t^2 \; t \; c]$ no variable may be eliminated after t^3. For, with the latter specification $\xi_i < \xi_\alpha$, for $i = t^2, t, c$. So the models $Q[t, c]$, $Q[t^2, c]$ and $Q[t^2, t]$ are indeed not admitted. They are included in N, as is evident from the fifth column of Table V.2. On the basis of the relative standard errors of $Q[t^3 \; t \; c]$ the inadmissability of $Q[t \; c]$ is once more evident but also that of $Q[t^3 \; c]$ and of $Q[t^3 \; t]$. However, model $Q[t^3 \; t^2]$ cannot be rejected in any way – indeed, there is no significant autocorrelation either – and so model $Q[t^3 \; t^2]$ is the only admitted model with 2 variables.

Since the values ξ_i to $Q[t^3 \; t^2]$ are larger than the critical ξ_α the models $Q[t^3]$ and $Q[t^2]$ would be admitted but for the fact that in this case the computed value d is lower than the critical bound. On this ground model $Q[c]$ is also rejected, although this happens by means of a von Neumann ratio. However, the autocorrelation of model $Q[t]$ appears to be non-significant.

As it is, $Q[t]$ has not yet been tested on its zerocoefficients. Since none of the models $Q[t^3 \; t]$, $Q[t^2 \; t]$ and $Q[t, c]$ are admitted, no $S(2)$ can be found on the basis of which $Q[t]$ can be tested. However, testing of $Q[t]$ on the basis of a specification with 3 explanatory variables $S(3)$ might lead to the rejection of the hypothesis that 2 coefficients may be assumed 0 at the same time. We shall perform the test on the basis of $Q[t^2 \; t \; c]$.

This takes place by means of a variance analysis. We calculate

$$\phi = [\hat{\beta}_2 \; \hat{\beta}_0] \left\{ \begin{bmatrix} 1 & & \\ & 0 & \\ & & 1 \end{bmatrix} (X'X)^{-1} \begin{bmatrix} 1 & & \\ & 0 & \\ & & 1 \end{bmatrix} \right\}^{-1} \begin{bmatrix} \hat{\beta}_2 \\ \hat{\beta}_0 \end{bmatrix}$$

in which $\hat{\beta}_2$ and $\hat{\beta}_0$ are the computed regression coefficients of t^2 and c in $Q[t^2 \; t \; c]$ and $X'X$ is the moments matrix with $X = [t^2 \; t \; c]$. So, to compute ϕ we only need the relevant rows and columns of $(X'X)^{-1}$, namely the first and the third ones. In this respect model $Q[t]$ is admitted if

$$\phi < 2s^2 \; F_{0.05}(2.15)$$

TABLE V.2

Analysis of the group of models that can be derived from $Q[t^3\ t^2\ t\ c]$

100 ξ				ξ_α[d]	d	d_L	N/A[e]	R[e]
t^3	t^2	t	c					
79	57	154	371	46.6	1.51	0.82	A	
–	39	35	42	46.9	1.51	0.93	A	R
41	–	35	46	46.9	1.50	0.93	A	R
42	40	–	68	46.9	1.43	0.93	A	R
69	79	129	–	46.9	1.32	0.84[a]	A	
–	–	74	172	47.2	1.10	1.05	N	
–	48	–	54	47.2	1.24	1.05	N	
–	109	75	–	47.2		0.95[a]	N	
243	–	–	161	47.2	1.01	1.05	N	
87	–	56	–	47.2	1.15	0.95	N	
54	48	–	–	47.2	1.25	0.95[a]	A	R
88				47.4	0.99	1.06[a]	N	
	68			47.4	1.03	1.06[a]	N	
		56		47.4	1.08	1.06[a]	A	R
			81	47.4	1.06[b]	1.32[c]	N	

[a] Critical lower bound d_L according to Kramer (1970) at the 90% level.
[b] Van Neumann ratio.
[c] Critical lower bound according to Hart (1942) at the 90% level.
[d] Critical lower bound defined as the reciprocal of Student's **t** variable at the 95% level. Cf. Pearson and Hartley (1966, p. 146, Table 12, column 6).
[e] N = not admitted, A = admitted, R = relevant.

in which s^2 is the estimated variance of model $Q[t^2\ t\ c]$. The computed value of ϕ is here 5.0192 and proves to be smaller than the largest admissable value at the 95% level, viz. 5.3724. So model $Q[t]$ is not rejected.

We could also perform the same test on the basis of $Q[t^3\ t\ c]$. In that case too $Q[t]$ turns out to be admitted ($3.83 < 5.52$). We could finally test $Q[t]$ on the basis of $Q[t^3\ t^2\ t]$ or even against $Q[t^3\ t^2\ t\ c]$. In an approach on a small scale, as we have here, the required calculations can take place in a simple way, although it will often prove to be unnecessary. With an approach as described in Chapter IV the 2 last-mentioned tests are not carried out. According to point 5 on page 71 a simultaneous test is only applied when 2 or more coefficients of a specification are significantly different from 0. In Table V.2 this is the case with $Q[t^2\ t\ c]$ and

$Q[t^3\ t\ c]$, so that, also in the procedure according to Chapter IV, only the 2 tests that were actually carried out above would have been applied[6]. If one of the tests would have given a negative result, this would already have been a sufficient reason to refer $Q[t]$ to N. So this has not happened in our situation.

Out of the 7 admitted models 5 prove to be relevant. Model $Q[t^3\ t^2\ t\ c]$ has 2 values of ξ_i larger than 1 and consequently, on the ground of Lemma 5, it has a larger forecasting interval than the admitted models $Q[t^3\ t^2\ t]$ and $Q[t^3\ t^2\ c]$. The latter model has in its turn a larger forecasting interval than $Q[t^3\ t^2]$ that has been admitted too. Now the forecasting interval of the selection indicator $\det\theta\hat{\Omega}$ of the 5 relevant and admitted models is determined. With forecasts for 1 year and 1 variable, so $m=1$ and $\tau=1$ (4.3) and (3.41) give the formula

$$\det\theta\hat{\Omega} = s^2(1+q)\,F_\alpha(1, T-k).$$

The interval is then

$$\frac{-\sqrt{s^2(1+q)\,F_\alpha}}{2} \leqslant \mathbf{e}_t \leqslant \frac{\sqrt{s^2(1+q)\,F_\alpha}}{2}.$$

For the years 1966 and 1967 taken separately, Table V.3 gives the intervals of the 5 relevant and admitted models in increasing order.
Column 2 of Table V.3 gives a measure for the goodness of fit of the model in the past, the columns 3 and 4 for the degree of divergency of the development of the exogeneous variables in the future and column 5 for the degree of simplicity of the forecasting procedure.

TABLE V.3

The forecasting intervals of the admitted and relevant models of table V.2 (1966 and 1967 separately)

Model	s^2	q 1966	q 1967	$F(1, T-k)$	Width of interval 1966[a]	Width of interval 1967
$Q[t]$	0.9393	0.1712	0.1897	4.45	4.425	4.460
$Q[t^2\ t\ c]$	0.7299	0.6299	0.9550	4.54	4.650	5.100
$Q[t^3\ t\ c]$	0.7480	0.8064	1.3473	4.54	4.950	5.650
$Q[t^3\ t^2]$	0.8659	0.8839	1.5374	4.49	5.410	6.280
$Q[t^3\ t^2\ c]$	0.8085	0.9988	1.8311	4.54	5.420	6.450

[a] $2\sqrt{\text{column 2} \times (1+\text{column 3}) \times \text{column 5}} \times 1000$. The unit is billions of guilders.

Model $Q[t]$ gives the smallest forecasting interval, both for 1966 and for 1967, in spite of the worst fit. Model $Q[t^2 \ t \ c]$ comes second, because of the good fit, but also due to a not so very large value of q. So here the value of q plays an important part in the selection. As it has been mentioned previously,[7] due to their smaller q value linear trends in linear models have a certain lead. Table V.4 shows that with the selected functions of time the value of q increases with the number of variables, with the length of the forecasting period and with the exponent of the trend.

TABLE V.4

Some values of q

	$Q[t]$	$Q[t\ c]$	$Q[t^2\ t\ c]$	$Q[t^3\ t^2]$	$Q[t^3\ t^2\ t\ c]$
1966	0.1712	0.2418	0.6299	0.8839	1.3905
1967	0.1897	0.2831	0.9550	1.5374	2.9798
1968	0.2091	0.3285	1.4020	2.6020	5.8603
1969	0.2295	0.3781	1.9964	4.1436	10.7038
1970	0.2508	0.4317	2.7661	6.3538	18.4012

Since, with forecasts for the separate years, model $Q[t]$ is to be preferred, both for 1966 and for 1967, it need not be surprising that this model gives also the best forecast when one selects according to simultaneous intervals.

We only compare the best 2 models. According to (3.46) with $m=1$ and $\tau>1$ the simultaneous variance-covariance matrix is

$$\hat{\Omega} = s^2 [M + I_\tau]$$

and so

$$\det \theta\hat{\Omega} = (s^2\theta)^\tau \det [M + I_\tau]$$

It is most practical to take $\sqrt[\tau]{\det\theta\hat{\Omega}}$ as a standard here, which leads to

$$s^2\theta\sqrt{\det(M + I_\tau)} \tag{5.1}$$

for $\tau=2$.

The value of s^2 has already been given in Table V.3. The value of θ increases. We get $\theta=7.7138$ for model $Q[t]$ against 8.0143 for model $Q[t^2 \ t \ c]$. The values for $\sqrt{\det(M+I_\tau)}$ are 1.1665 and 1.6226 respectively, so that (5.1) gives a value of 8.4520 billions for $Q[t]$ against 9.4334 for

$Q[t^2\ t\ c]$. From this it appears that $Q[t]$ is also preferable for 1966 and 1967 together. So the simultaneous consideration has little to add here to the comparison per year. We conclude that for the simultaneous forecast of the export surplus in 1966 and 1967 we choose the procedure that is optimal with repect to $Q[t]$, viz.

$$Q_t = 0.0380\ t$$

The result, given as a point-estimate in millions of guilders is $Q_{66} = 720$ and $Q_{67} = 760$. When the results are given as a 95% probability interval we get in millions of guilders[8]

$$-1490 \leqslant \mathbf{Q}_{66} \leqslant 2930$$
$$-1470 \leqslant \mathbf{Q}_{67} \leqslant 2990.$$

5.2.2. *Some Problems*

As model $Q[t]$ dominates over the other 4 admitted models we have no problem of choice here. However, sometimes we find that model i is better for the forecasting of year τ_1 but model j is better for the forecasting of year τ_2. If a forecast must be given for both years, the simultaneous forecasting interval is decisive, at least if – like in this book – non-linear models with variable coefficients are not admitted.

Say e.g. that according to the tests executed $Q[t]$ would not have been admitted, but $Q[t\ c]$ would. In that case model $Q[t^2\ t\ c]$ appears to have the smallest interval for 1966, viz. 4650 million against 4670 million for model $Q[t\ c]$, but the situation is reversed for 1967, viz. 4750 million for $Q[t\ c]$ against 5100 million for $Q[t^2\ t\ c]$. If one considers a good forecast equally important in both years, the indicator $\det \theta\hat{\Omega}$ is decisive. If one wishes to have the importance of a good forecast in either year count, we select according to trace $\theta\hat{\Omega}W\sqrt{\det\theta\hat{\Omega}}$ – see (3.68) – when a quadratic loss-function is used and according to trace $W\sqrt{\theta\hat{\Omega}}\ \sqrt{\det\theta\hat{\Omega}}$ – see (3.70) and (3.78) – when the absolute values of the forecasting errors are weighted. We give the calculations in full below.

Calculations of the simultaneous forecasting interval for 1966 and 1967 for the models $Q[t\ c]$ and $Q[t^2\ t\ c]$.

If the choice were to be between the models $Q[t\ c]$ and $Q[t^2\ t\ c]$ the conclusion would be:

	$Q[t\ c]$	$Q[t^2\ t\ c]$
s^2	0.9774	0.7299
$X'X$	$\begin{bmatrix} 18 & 171 \\ 171 & 2109 \end{bmatrix}$	$\begin{bmatrix} 18 & 171 & 2109 \\ 171 & 2109 & 29241 \\ 2109 & 29241 & 432345 \end{bmatrix}$
X_τ	$\begin{bmatrix} 1 & 1 \\ 19 & 20 \end{bmatrix}$	$\begin{bmatrix} 1 & 1 \\ 19 & 20 \\ 361 & 400 \end{bmatrix}$
$M = X'_\tau(X'X)^{-1}X_\tau$	$\begin{bmatrix} 0.2418 & 0.2614 \\ 0.2614 & 0.2831 \end{bmatrix}$	$\begin{bmatrix} 0.6299 & 0.7654 \\ 0.7654 & 0.9550 \end{bmatrix}$
$\hat{\Omega} = s^2[M+I]$	$\begin{bmatrix} 1.2137 & 0.2555 \\ 0.2555 & 1.2541 \end{bmatrix}$	$\begin{bmatrix} 1.1897 & 0.5587 \\ 0.5587 & 1.4270 \end{bmatrix}$
$F(2, T-k)$	3.68	3.74
$\theta = \dfrac{2(T-k)}{T-k-1} F(2, T-k)$	7.8507	8.0143
$\theta\hat{\Omega}$	$\begin{bmatrix} 9.5284 & 2.0059 \\ 2.0059 & 9.8450 \end{bmatrix}$	$\begin{bmatrix} 9.5346 & 4.4776 \\ 4.4776 & 11.4364 \end{bmatrix}$
$\det \theta\hat{\Omega}$	89.7888	88.9926
$\sqrt{\det \theta\hat{\Omega}}$	9.4757	9.4336
$\operatorname{trace} W\theta\hat{\Omega}\sqrt{\det \theta\hat{\Omega}}$	$90.2884w_1 + 93.2941w_2$	$89.9455w_1 + 107.8864w_2$
$[w_1\tilde{s}_1 + w_2\tilde{s}_2]\sqrt{\det \theta\hat{\Omega}}$	$29.2496w_1 + 29.7319w_2$	$29.1291w_1 + 31.9016w_2$

Check: $\sqrt{\det \theta\hat{\Omega}} = \sqrt{\det \theta s^2[M+I]} = \theta s^2 \sqrt{\det[M+I]}$

$s^2\theta$	7.6733	5.8496
$\sqrt{\det[M+I]}$	1.2349	4.6226
$\sqrt{\det \theta\hat{\Omega}}$	9.4759	9.4334

(a) If no weighing is used $Q[t^2\ t\ c]$ is chosen. It has the smallest value of $\sqrt{\det \theta\hat{\Omega}}$.

(b) If one calculates with a quadratic loss function $\mathbf{e}'_t W \mathbf{e}_t$, $Q[t^2\ t\ c]$ is only chosen if the damage due to a wrong forecast in 1967 is less than $2\frac{1}{2}\%$ of that of 1966. For, the value of trace $\theta W\hat{\Omega}\sqrt{\det \theta\hat{\Omega}}$ is only smaller than the corresponding value of model $Q[t\ c]$ if

$$w_2 < 0.0238\ w_1 .$$

(c) If one weighs according to absolute forecasting errors, the critical margin is

$$w_2 < 0.0556\, w_1 .$$

It will be clear that in this situation one will generally attach a lower value to w_2 than to w_1, as it is possible to adjust the economy when new information makes it evident that the forecast is incorrect or improbable. On the other hand, the rigidity of the impact of policy measures is such, that it is doubtful whether it is permissable to attach an almost negligible value to the weight. If the minimum value of w_2 would be fixed at $w_2 = 0.1\, w_1$, yet $Q\,[t \;\; c]$ would have been preferable if this model had not been set aside for being unreliable on the ground of the reference period.

It must finally be remarked that it is possible that model i is better for the year τ_1 and model j better for the year τ_2 and that yet no pair of positive weights can be found that levels the weighted simultaneous forecasting interval of both models. The solution of this paradox is to be found in the fact that the weights are of importance only for the forecasting errors that are yet to be made, but not for those that have already been made. One might e.g. count errors that lie further back in the past less heavily than recent errors. One may then introduce a non-singular matrix W with evaluations for residuals and combinations of them for each of the T years of the past. One would then obtain a forecasting procedure in which $\hat{\Pi}$ is replaced by

$$\Pi^* = Y'W^{-1}X\,[X'W^{-1}X]^{-1}$$

with corresponding estimated variance-covariance matrix of forecasting errors $\hat{\Omega}^*$. For $W = I_T$ we then get $\hat{\Omega}^* = \hat{\Omega}$ and for W singular the problem must be formulated with a shorter reference period.

5.3. The forecast of the export surplus one year in advance

5.3.1. *Introduction*

It is obvious that with forecasting periods of one year only a much larger number of variables can be used than with larger forecasting periods. However, also here we shall restrict ourselves to a discussion of a number of groups that illustrate certain aspects of the selection problem. 5 groups will be introduced. Table V.5 gives a survey of them. We shall deal with

TABLE V.5

The set of models for the forecast of the export surplus Q_t in 1966

No.	Explanatory variables										Idem conditional		Relevant and admitted
	const	t	t^2	t^3	Q_{-1}	Q_{-2}	B_{-1}	M_{-1}	Y_{-1}	$\tilde{w}_{-1}$	$\mathbf{b}_c$	$\tilde{\mathbf{w}}$	
1[a]	×	×	×	×									
2	×	×	×										R
3	×	×		×									R
4	×		×	×									R
5		×	×	×									
6	×	×											
7	×		×										
8		×	×										
9		×		×									
10	×			×									
11			×	×									R
12				×									
13			×										
14		×											R
15	×												
16[a]	×				×	×							
17					×	×							
18	×				×								R
19	×					×							R
20						×							
21					×								R
22[a]	×						×	×					
23							×	×					R
24	×						×						
25	×							×					R
26							×						R
27								×					
28[a]	×			×					×				
29	×								×				
30				×					×				R
31									×				R
32[a]					×					×			R
33										×			R
36[b]				×							×	×	R
37[b]				×								×	

[a] Functions as a truncated maximum specification.

[b] Conditional.

this table as if we were dealing with a number of truncated maximum-specifications $S_i[T-1]$. To be true, the $T-1$ has been replaced by a smaller number to get a clear survey, but the analysis takes place analogously. We have already discussed the first group in Section 5.2. The others will have their turn here. In Subsection 5.3.2 the group with exclusively lagged process-variables. In Subsection 5.3.3 the group $Q[B_{-1}\ M_{-1}\ c]$ with only exogeneous explanatory variables. The group $Q[Y_{-1}\ Q_{-1}\ c]$ links up with the simultaneous forecast of Y and Q in Section 5.5. In Subsection 5.3.5 the last group of only 2 models is discussed and there we also select the optimal forecasting procedure from the models of Table V.5. We continue with a passage about conditional models in Subsection 5.3.6 and finally in Subsection 5.3.7 we do not resist the temptation to investigate how the optimal forecasting procedure would have performed in the sixties.

5.3.2. *Models with Lagged Endogeneous Variables*

As explained in Section 4.5 the characteristics of the least squares estimates are approximatively valid here ,when we are dealing with forecasts based on observations, that is for forecasts 1 year in advance when Q_{-1} is the explanatory variable, etc. So we can once more construct a table with the relative standard errors and Durbin-Watson statistics (see Table V.6.). Model $Q[Q_{-2}]$ appears to be inadmissable due to the relative

TABLE V.6

Analysis of the group that can be derived from $Q[Q_{-1}\ Q_{-2}\ c]$

$100\,\xi$			ξ_α	d	d_L	N/A [c]	R [c]
Q_{-1}	Q_{-2}	c					
52	104	76	46.30	1.84	0.86	A	
43	133		46.62	1.82	0.87 [a]	A	
51		77	46.93	1.68	1.01	A	R
	1140	56	46.62	1.23	0.98	A	R [d]
8			47.17	1.82	1.02 [a]	A	R
	204		46.93	1.13	0.99 [a]	N	
		81	47.39	1.06	1.32 [b]	N	

[a] Critical lower bound d_L according to Kramer (1970) at the 90 % level.
[b] Von Neumann ratio.
[c] N = non-admitted, A = admitted, R = relevant.
[d] See text.

standard error of 43% of the coefficient of Q_{-1} in $Q[Q_{-1}\ Q_{-2}]$. For the rest, $Q[c]$ is not admitted[9], both because of the zerocoefficient in the first column and because of the low von Neumann ratio.

Out of the 5 admitted models $Q[Q_{-1}\ Q_{-2}\ c]$ and $Q[Q_{-1}\ Q_{-2}]$ are not relevant because of the high standard error in the 2nd column. Also in $Q[Q_{-2}\ c]$ the coefficient of Q_{-2} has a high standard error. However, it is not possible to eliminate Q_{-2} from this model, because then one ends up with the inadmissable model $Q[c]$. Certainly one might be able by roundabout methods to declare $Q[Q_{-2}\ c]$ non-relevant but in a case like the underlying one it is easier to include $Q[Q_{-2}\ c]$ in the calculations of the intervals. It will drop out automatically should it be non-relevant. The forecasting intervals for 1966 of the three relevant admitted models are in millions of guilders:

$Q[Q_{-1}]$	3720
$Q[Q_{-1}\ c]$	3770
$Q[Q_{-2}\ c]$	4400

These intervals are smaller than those of group 1 (see Table V.3). However, there are more groups to come.

It must be noted that the standard errors of the model have been computed according to the usual formulas with exogeneous variables. However, with the calculation of the standard errors of $Q[Q_{-1}\ c]$ according to a formula by Shenton and Johnson (1965) the difference turned out to be negligible. This provided no cause to change the existing procedure. For the rest, one should add to this that it is apparent from certain simulations that Shenton and Johnson's approximation formula converges less rapidly as has been assumed[10]. It has also been investigated here how model $Q[Q_{-1}]$ would have behaved with forecasts for 1967 and later. As we have said for forecasting periods of more than 1 year the optimal forecasting procedure of these models cannot be determined upon so easily. It has been suggested in Section 4.5 to use

$$\hat{Q}_{t+\tau-1} = \beta^{\tau} Q_{t-1}$$

and for the variance of the forecasting error

$$\operatorname{var} \mathbf{e}_{t+\tau} \approx qs^2 [(1+\tau)\, \hat{\boldsymbol{\beta}}^{\tau}]^2 + [\hat{\beta}^{2\tau} + \cdots + \hat{\beta}^2 + 1]\, s^2 .$$

Given the values of model $Q[Q_{-1}]$, namely $s^2=0.7688$, $\hat{\beta}=0.4819$ and $q=0.0041$ the result is

	τ	var $\mathbf{e}_{t+\tau}$ (billions of guilders)^2	Interval millions of guilders
1966	0	0.7720	3.720
1967	1	0.9504	4.130
1968	2	0.9903	4.220
1969	3	0.9991	4.235
1970	4	1.0010	4.240
1971	5	1.0013	4.240
1972	6	1.0014	4.240

So, also for 1967 $Q[Q_{-1}]$ appears to have a smaller forecasting interval than the models of group 1.

According to Section 4.5 yet another – simpler – approximation of the forecasting interval of $Q[Q_{-1}]$ can be given by increasing the estimation of β a little, and neglecting the stochasticity of this $\hat{\boldsymbol{\beta}}^*$. For, the variance of $\hat{\boldsymbol{\beta}}^*$ is less important than that of $\mathbf{Q}_{t+\tau-1}$, because the latter gives a cumulation of yearly disturbances. To illustrate this we have computed the forecasting intervals of the stochast

$$\mathbf{u}_t = \mathbf{Q}_t - 0.5\mathbf{Q}_{t-1} \cong N(\alpha, \sigma^2).$$

$\hat{\boldsymbol{\beta}}$ has been augmented from 0.4819 to 0.5. The forecasting interval of $\mathbf{Q}_{t+\tau}$, computed according to the formula

$$2\sqrt{s^2 F(1, 17) \sum_{i=0}^{\tau-1} (0.5)^{2i}}$$

then becomes 3750 million for 1966 and 4470 million for 1967. So this is already larger than the intervals of $Q[Q_{-1}]$, in spite of the slight increase of $\hat{\boldsymbol{\beta}}$. Therefore, a rapid and fair approximation can be obtained this way. All things considered, the forecasting procedure

$$Q_{t+1} = (0.4819)^2\, Q_{t-1}$$

gives a smaller interval for 1967 than the models of Section 5.2. If one would make forecasts with this procedure for two consecutive years, the result would give a smaller estimated forecasting interval, viz.

1966: $\hat{Q}_t = 125$ million
$-1730 \leqslant Q_t \leqslant 1990$ (million)

1967: $\hat{Q}_t = 60$ million
$-2000 \leqslant Q_t \leqslant 2120$ (million).

5.3.3. *Models with Lagged Exogeneous Variables*

In case of models with lagged exogeneous variables an interval can be given for 1966, if the lag is not shorter than 1 year. Therefore, there are no special problems in this section. Model $Q[B_{-1}\ \ M_{-1}\ \ c]$ uses the component parts of Q, namely the export B_t and the import M_t. It is apparent from Table V.7 that apart from $Q[c]$ all models are admitted. Only 3 of them are relevant. Their intervals are also set forth in Table V.7.

5.3.4. *Models that can be derived from* $Q\ [Y_{-1}\ \ Q_{-1}\ \ c]$

A special feature of the selection presents itself with the group of models that can be derived from $Q[Y_{-1}\ \ Q_{-1}\ \ c]$, in which Y represents

TABLE V.7

Analysis of the group that can be derived from $Q[B_{-1}\ \ M_{-1}\ \ c]$

100 ξ			ξ_α	d	d_L	N/A [c]	R [c]	Forecasting interval 1966
B_{-1}	M_{-1}	c						Millions of guilders
54	57	282	46.62	1.88	0.90	A		
53	57		46.93	1.83	0.91 [a]	A	R	4060
137		4698	46.93	1.26	1.01	A		
	206	443	46.93	1.24	1.01	A		
51			47.17	1.26	1.02 [a]	A	R	4260
	54		47.17	1.23	1.02 [a]	A	R	4320
		81	47.89	1.06	1.32 [b]	N		

[a] Critical lower bound according to Kramer (1970) at the 90 % level.
[b] Von Neumann ratio.
[c] N = non-admitted, A = admitted, R = relevant.

Gross National Product. Written in full the model is

$$\mathbf{Q}_t = \beta Q_{-1} + \gamma Y_{-1} + \alpha + \mathbf{u}_t$$

with $\mathbf{u}_t \cong N(0, \sigma^2)$

This model can also be formulated as

$$\mathbf{Q}_t = -\beta X_{-1} + (\gamma - \beta) Y_{-1} + \alpha + \mathbf{u}_t$$

in which X_t represents Gross Domestic Expenditures. So this model uses also the component parts of Q_t, although in another sense than in the previous section. In Table V.8 only the first specification of the model is included. So a model such as $Q[X_{-1}]$ remains outside the set-up.

TABLE V.8

Analysis of the group that can be derived from $Q[Q_{-1}\ Y_{-1}\ c]$

100 ξ								
Q_{-1}	Y_{-1}	c	ξ_α	d	d_L	N/A[c]	R[c]	Forecasting interval
54	1060	209	46.62	1.90	0.90	A		
54	84		46.93	1.84	0.91[a]	A	R	4090
51		77	46.93	1.68	1.01	A	R[d]	3770
	246	402	46.93	1.24	1.01	A		
8			47.17	1.82	1.02[a]	A	R[d]	3720
	55		47.17	1.23	1.02[a]	A	R	4350
		81	47.39	1.06	1.32[b]	N		

[a] Critical lower bound according to Kramer (1970) at the 90% level.
[b] Von Neumann ratio.
[c] N = non-admitted, A = admitted, R = relevant.
[d] Already discussed in Table V.6

It is apparent from Table V.8 that there are 6 admitted models, 4 of which are relevant. Moreover, it appears that $Q[Q_{-1}\ c]$ and $Q[Q_{-1}]$, that were considered earlier, need neither be rejected here. On the other hand, $Q[c]$ turned out to be in the set N already.

5.3.5. *The Specification $Q[Q_{-1}\ \tilde{w}_{-1}]$ and the Ranking of the Relevant Admitted Models*

We introduce the specification $Q[Q_{-1}\ \tilde{w}_{-1}]$ as a transition to the discussion of conditional models. In this specification $\tilde{w}$ represents the registered unemployment as a percentage of the Labour force. The results of the calculations can be found in Table V.9. The latter table is selfevident.

TABLE V.9

Analysis of the group that can be derived from $Q\,[Q_{-1}\ \tilde{w}_{-1}]$

100 ξ		ξ_α	d	d_L[a]		Interval in millions of guilders
Q_{-1}	$\tilde{w}_{-1}$					
58	59	46.93	1.93	0.93	R	3560
8		47.17	1.82	1.02	R	3720
	42	47.17	1.26	1.02	R	3750

[a] Critical lower bound according to Kramer (1970) at the 90 % level.

Since there are no models that are admitted according to one table, but are not according to another, we can construct the set of relevant and admitted models, which is here the sum of the contributions of each table.

When we rank these models according to the size of their intervals we get Table V.10.

$$Q_t = 0.3535\, Q_{t-1} + 0.1491\, \tilde{w}_{-1}$$

turns out to be the best forecasting procedure for 1966. When making references we shall call this forecasting procedure *procedure A*.

The point estimate for 1966 is $\hat{Q}_{1966} = 240$ million and the 95% forecasting interval in millions of guilders

$$-1540 \leqslant Q_{66} \leqslant 2040\,.$$

This is a narrower interval than the one of Subsection 5.1.1. However, its horizon is also more limited.

5.3.6. *Conditional Forecasts*

In order to indicate how conditional forecasting intervals behave in this frame, we present model $Q\,[Q_{-1}\ \mathbf{b}_c]$. In doing so it has been assumed that the increase of world demand in 1966 is known. We have taken the variable $\mathbf{b}_c$ to represent world trade, defined as the percentual increase of the re-weighted world trade, as it is yearly published by the C.P.B.

The results of the regression are:

$$Q_t = \underset{(45\%)}{0.4739}Q_{t-1} + \underset{(673\%)}{0.0035}\mathbf{b}_{ct} \qquad d = 1.84\,.$$

TABLE V.10

The set of relevant admitted models according to the width of their forecasting intervals in 1966 (millions of guilders)

	P	Width of the interval	Position of the interval	
1	$Q[Q_{-1}\ \tilde{w}_{-1}]$	3560	−1540	2020
2	$Q[Q_{-1}]$	3720	−1730	1990
3	$Q[\tilde{w}_{-1}]$	3750	−1670	2080
4	$Q[Q_{-1}\ c]$	3770	−1500	2270
5	$Q[B_{-1}\ M_{-1}]$	4060	−1410	2650
6	$Q[Q_{-1}\ Y_{-1}]$	4090	−1430	2650
7	$Q[B_{-1}]$	4260	−1320	2940
8	$Q[M_{-1}]$	4320	−1380	2940
9	$Q[Y_{-1}]$	4350	−1390	2950
10	$Q[t]$	4425	−1490	2930
11	$Q[t^2\ t\ c]$	4650	−2800	1850
12	$Q[t^3\ t^2\ t\ c]$	4950	−3180	1770
13	$Q[t^3\ t^2]$	5410	−3220	2190
14	$Q[t^3\ t^2\ c]$	5420	−3670	1750

The relative standard error of 673% indicates that model $Q[Q_{-1}\ \mathbf{b}_c]$ is inferior to model $Q[Q_{-1}]$. So the fact that information about 1966 can be used does not help to obtain a smaller forecasting interval for Q_{1966}. For, should we insert for b_c the value 6.5 that was found afterwards, the interval for Q_t would be 3910 million in 1966 which would mean only a fifth place in Table V.10.

The second conditional model assumes that, apart from b_c in the year τ the degree of excess demand in the economy is also known. As a measure we use $\tilde{w}$, the unemployment percentage. This gives model $Q[Q_{-1}\ \mathbf{b}_c\ \tilde{w}]$.

The regression gives as a result

$$Q_t = 0.4869Q_{t-1} - 0.0619\mathbf{b}_{c_t} + 0.3610\tilde{\mathbf{w}}_t \qquad d = 2.05.$$
$$(33\%) \qquad (41\%) \qquad (28\%)$$

The negative sign of $\mathbf{b}_c$ expresses that with increasing world demand Dutch imports – especially because of stock formation – react more heavily than exports. With increasing stress of home demand – so decreasing $\tilde{w}_t$ – the export surplus decreases likewise, as is indicated by the positive sign of $\tilde{w}_t$. This is explained both by additional imports and by a retarded development of exports, due to a lack of capacity. When the stress lessens, the effect on imports is negative, while the increasing excess in the production capacity is partly filled up by an accellerated growth of exports (the so-called 'Zijlstra' effect).

The relation between Q_t and $\tilde{\mathbf{w}}$ is so close that knowledge about $\tilde{\mathbf{w}}$ is now clearly of consequence for the forecasting interval. With the values of $b_c=6.5$ and $\tilde{w}=1.2$ that were found afterwards the conditional interval of $Q\,[Q_{-1}\ \mathbf{b}_c\ \tilde{\mathbf{w}}]$ dives below the lowest computed value. For, the interval for 1966 becomes 2950 million. The size of the interval appears to be rather insensitive to small changes in the given conditional values. However, they do procure an effect on the point estimates, that is changes in the given values of $\tilde{w}_\tau$ do. Those in b_{c_τ} are neglible because of the small regressioncoefficient of this variable, so that $Q\,[Q_{-1}\ \tilde{\mathbf{w}}]$ differs only slightly from $Q\,[Q_{-1}\ \tilde{\mathbf{w}}\ \mathbf{b}_c]$ as far as forecasting interval and point estimate are concerned.

The conclusion we can draw from all this is that knowledge about $\tilde{\mathbf{w}}_t$ may contribute to the reduction of the forecasting interval of $\mathbf{Q}_t$. However, if $\tilde{\mathbf{w}}_\tau$ is only predicted because of its aid in the forecasting of $\mathbf{Q}_\tau$, it is better according to Lemma 2 to incorporate the explanatory variables of $\tilde{\mathbf{w}}_t$ directly in the analysis of $\mathbf{Q}_t$. Whatever the case may be, the conditional forecasts here suggest that better forecasts can probably be made if one searches for explanatory variables that are able to measure the degree of stress in the economy faster or better than w_{-1}. For the rest, it was through this conditional approach that the model $Q\,[Q_{-1}\ \tilde{w}_{-1}]$ mentioned before has come to the front.

5.3.7. *The Performance of Procedure A in the Sixties*

Although the groups of models discussed here were only meant to elucidate the selection method and did not pretend to give any actual application of the procedure, in the end we could not resist the temptation to investigate how procedure *A* would have performed compared with the existing forecasting methods. For the sake of a fair judgement a comparison between the forecasting interval of procedure *A* and the intervals of e.g. the models of the C.P.B. is desired. The latter models are mainly the following ones:

(a) The model by Verdoorn and van Eijk (1958) and its later versions, and

(b) The C.S. model by van den Beld (1968).

However, the calculation of the forecasting intervals of these models meets with the following problems:

(1) The models are non-linear.

(2) The reduced forms of both models contain more explanatory variables than observations, so that the forecasting intervals are indefinite.

(3) The calculation of the conditional intervals, which are based on the structural equations also calls for problems, as either there are too many explanatory variables left or the conditionality must also be extended to a number of coefficients that were chosen *a priori*, but only after the comparison with some alternatives.

It must finally be stated that the official forecasts of the C.P.B. are often not simply equal to the output of the models as all kinds of recent information may cause revisions. So in order to obtain a fair evaluation of the forecasting results of procedure A it is better to compare them with the unconditional forecasts of the C.P.B., i.e. with the forecasts as they are published in the yearly plans.

In order not to make the period of evaluation too short the following procedure has been used:

(1) Procedure A was recalculated on the basis of the reference period 1948–1960.

(2) It was assumed that the model involved would also be optimal on the basis of the shorter reference period.

(3) Q_t was predicted on the basis of the recalculated procedure for 1948–1960 and the realisations of the explanatory variables for the years 1960–1969 inc. So the estimates are not adjusted every time.

(4) The forecast of the C.P.B. for 1961–1970 inc. was taken from CEP (1961) to CEP (1970) inclusive.

(5) To compare the forecast of ad 3 and ad 4, a number of criteria was laid down, such as inequality coefficients, etc.

A regression of Q_t on Q_{t-1} and $\tilde{w}_{-1}$ gives for the period 1948–1960 inc. the following result

$$Q_t = 0.3691Q_{t-1} + 0.1503\tilde{w}_{-1} \qquad d = 1.95.$$
$$(70\%) \qquad\qquad (71\%)$$

This deviates only slightly from the result of Subsection 5.3.5. It is therefore plausible that this model was also among the best of the set of admitted models for the period 1948–1961.

To make a comparison, the result for the interrupted period 1922–1938, 1948–1967 was:

$$Q_t = 0.4528 Q_{t-1} + 0.0125 w_{-1} \qquad d = 1.86.$$
$$(32\,\%) \qquad (119\,\%)$$

It appears that for this longer reference period the selected forecasting procedure is no longer relevant, for

$$Q_t = 0.4667\, Q_{t-1} \qquad d = 1.84$$
$$(30\,\%)$$

gives a forecasting procedure with a smaller interval[11].

The forecasts made for 1 year ahead every time by using procedure *A* have been presented in Table V.11 (column 2). In column 4 the forecasts of the C.P.B. are given. We have further presented the realisations (column 3) and the forecasting errors attached to both forecasts (columns 5 and 6).

TABLE V.11

A comparison between the forecasting errors of procedure *A* and the C.P.B. forecasts.
(billions of guilders)

t	$\hat{Q}$	Q	$\hat{Q}_{\text{C.P.B.}}$	e	$e_{\text{C.P.B.}}$
1961	0.69	0.70	−1.11	−0.01	−1.81
1962	0.43	0.63	0.71	−0.20	+0.08
1963	0.38	0.29	0.70	+0.09	+0.41
1964	0.26	−0.55	−1.02	+0.81	−0.47
1965	−0.07	0.28	−0.04	−0.35	−0.32
1966	0.25	−0.49	0.53	+0.74	+1.02
1967	−0.00	0.08	0.73	−0.08	+0.65
1968	0.39	0.59	0.77	−0.20	+0.18
1969	0.55	0.33	0.50	+0.22	+0.17
1970	0.38	−1.50	0.30	+1.88	+1.80
$\sum_t e_t^2$				5.0036	8.5381

Table V.11 shows that the sum of the squares of the forecasting errors of procedure *A* for the period 1961–1970 inc. is lower than the inequality coefficient of the C.P.B. forecasts. This is mainly caused by the large forecasting error of the C.P.B. in 1961. When we exclude that year, the figures are 5.0035 for procedure *A* and 5.2620 for the C.P.B.

The turningpoints can be analysed with the help of Figure V.1. The C.P.B. predicted 6 times the correct sign of Q_t. On one occasion (1964) this meant a prediction of a negative surplus. According to procedure A a negative surplus can only be predicted if the realisation of Q_{t-1} is negative. So with this procedure a turningpoint from + to − cannot be predicted. Since there are 3 of these turningpoints (1964, 1966 and 1970) procedure A is bound to predict a wrong sign at least 3 times. There are in fact 4 errors in sign, as the shift from − to + in 1965 was not predicted. In 1967 a surplus 0 was predicted instead of a positive surplus.

If one considers a positive surplus as favourable and a negative surplus as unfavourable, procedure A appears to be too optimistic as often as it is too pessimistic, whereas the C.P.B. was too optimistic 6 times out of 10, among which were the 5 latter years of the period.

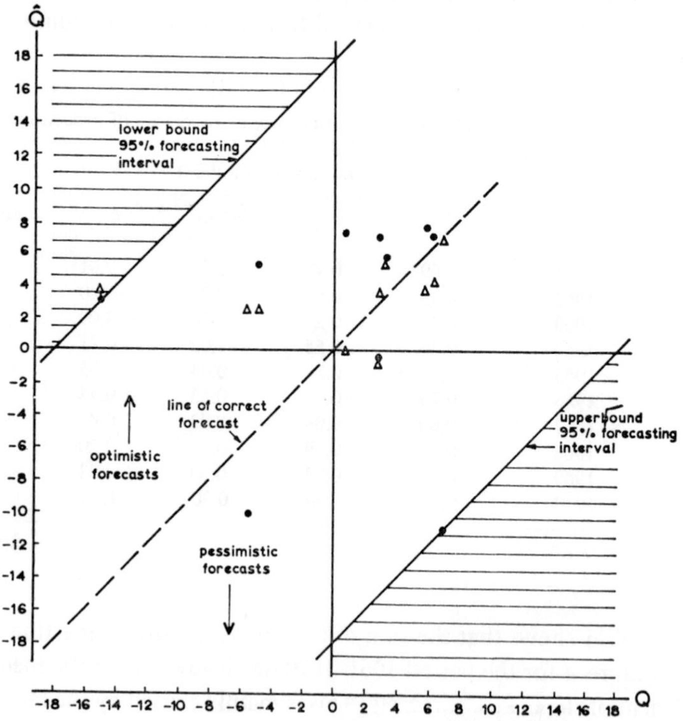

Fig. V.1. Forecast and realisation 1961–1970 × 100 millions of guilders. △ = forecast according to procedure A; ● = forecast according to C.P.B.

It can finally be examined whether the forecasting errors of procedure A have indeed remained inside the indicated forecasting interval. The interval has not been recalculated for the period 1948–1960 and neither has it been recalculated for each year according to the value of q_t. Due to the increase of the number of observations the forecasting interval becomes smaller, provided the new observations do not lie too far away from the computed regression line. Moreover, the forecasting interval changes with the degree of eccentricity of Q_{-1} and $\tilde{w}_{-1}$[12]. However, if we take the interval for 1966 as a rough indicator, the forecasting error must not be larger than 1.78 billion in absolute value. Evaluated according to this criterion the forecast for 1970 is too optimistic. In a situation like that there is every reason to look for a new procedure.

5.4. The Forecast of the Gross National Product

As a transition to the simultaneous forecast of $\mathbf{Q}_t$ and $\mathbf{Y}_t$ a paragraph has been inserted here about the forecast of the Gross National Product in 1966 on the basis of data from 1948–1965 inc.

3 Groups together including 25 models have been calculated, viz.

$Y\,[t^3\ t^2\ t\ c]$	with $16 - 1$	$= 15$	models
$Y\,[Y_{-1}\ Y_{-2}\ c]$	with $8 - 1 - 1 =$	6	models
$Y\,[Y_{-1}\ Q_{-1}\ c]$	with $8 - 1 - 3 =$	4	models
		25	models

The subtracted numbers relate to model $Y[\ ]$ and the models counted more than once. 7 models appear to be admitted, only 2 of which are relevant.

Admitted but not relevant were

$$Y\,[Y_{-1}\ Y_{-2}\ c]$$
$$Y\,[Y_{-1}\qquad c]$$
$$Y\,[Y_{-1}\ Y_{-2}\ \ ]$$
$$Y\,[Y_{-1}\ Q_{-1}\ c]$$
$$Y\,[Y_{-1}\ Q_{-1}\ \ ]$$

The relevant admitted models with their forecasting intervals for 1966 are:

$Y\,[Y_{-1}]$	6960 millions of guilders
$Y\,[t^3\ t^2\ t\ c]$	8430 millions of guilders.

The optimal forecasting procedure for 1966 is then

$$\hat{Y} = 1.0972 Y_{-1}$$

hence the forecast is

$$\hat{Y}_t = 75.70 \text{ billion}$$

with the interval in billions of guilders

$$72.22 \leqslant \mathbf{Y}_{1966} \leqslant 79.18\,.$$

5.5. The simultaneous forecast of Y_t and Q_t

5.5.1

When both the export surplus and G.N.P. are to be forecasted, the model must contain 2 equations according to Lemma 2. So $m=2$. As there exists an exact linear relation between $\mathbf{Y}_t$, $\mathbf{Q}_t$ and $\mathbf{X}_t$, namely $\mathbf{Y}_t - \mathbf{X}_t = \mathbf{Q}_t$, in which $\mathbf{X}_t$ represents the Gross expenditures, the models in $\mathbf{Q}_t$ and $\mathbf{Y}_t$ give a forecast for $\mathbf{X}_t$ at the same time. However, when $\mathbf{Y}_t$ and $\mathbf{Q}_t$ are the required variables, then, according to our analysis, the comparison of the models must indeed take place in $\mathbf{Y}_t$ and $\mathbf{Q}_t$, and not e.g. in $\mathbf{Y}_t$ and $\mathbf{X}_t$ from which $\mathbf{Q}_t$ is calculated afterwards.

Instead of starting with a maximumspecification again we merely give an illustration by means of a small group, in this case 7 models. In this group $QY[Q_{-1}\ \ Y_{-1}\ \ c]$ plays the part of the maximum specification. For the disturbances we assume

$$\mathbf{u}_t = \begin{bmatrix} \mathbf{u}_{1t} \\ \mathbf{u}_{2t} \end{bmatrix} \cong N\,[0, \Sigma]$$

for all t in which Σ is a constant non-singular 2×2 matrix. The model $QY[Q_{-1}\ \ Y_{-1}\ \ c]$ contains 3 explanatory variables. Through elimination of variables, i.e. assuming zero columns, $2^3-1=7$ models can be obtained. These are mentioned in Table V.12.

TABLE V.12

Computed and critical F-values for the models derived from $QY[Q_{-1}\ Y_{-1}\ c]$

Model number	Variable						
	Y_{-1}	Q_{-1}	c	F_α [a]	F_0 [b]	[c]	
1	927.59	1.66	0.26	3.81	0.16	A	R
2		×	×	3.74	0.15	N	
3	6693.56	2.47		3.74	0.15	A	R
4	1036.48		0.35	3.74	0.15	A	R
5	$\boxed{\times}$			3.68	0.14	A	R
6		×		3.68	0.14	N	
7			×	3.68	0.14	N	

[a] Critical lower bound for calculated F.
[b] Critical upper bound for the judgement of relevancy.
[c] N = non-admitted, A = admitted, R = relevant.

Least squares applied to both equations renders the following coefficients

	Q_{-1}	Y_{-1}	c
Q	0.4069	−0.0002	0.2868
Y	−0.2492	1.1197	−0.7714

and the matrix of residual sums of squares

$$E'E = \begin{bmatrix} 11.0617 & -9.9553 \\ -9.9553 & 33.3571 \end{bmatrix}.$$

The testing on zerocoefficients according to (4.33) requires also the diagonal elements of the matrix $(X'X)^{-1}$. These are the values r_i, given below. The teststatistic (4.34) can easiest be computed here through

$$\frac{P'_{.i}(E'E)^* P_{.i}}{r \det E'E} \times \frac{T - k - m + 1}{m}$$

in which $(E'E)^*$ is the adjoint matrix of $E'E$, so

$$E'E^* = \begin{bmatrix} 33.3571 & 9.9553 \\ 9.9553 & 11.0617 \end{bmatrix}$$

$\det E'E = 269.8784$.

Hence:

(1)	(2)	(3)	(4)	(5)	(6)	(7)
i	Variable	$P'_{.i}(E'E)^{*}P_{.i}$	r_i	$r_i \det E'E$	(3):(5)	$(6)\times\frac{T-k-m+1}{m}$
1	Q_{-1}	4.1903	0.0607	16.3816	0.2558	1.6627
2	Y_{-1}	13.8648	0.0036	0.0972	142.7060	927.59
3	c	4.9208	0.4532	122.3008	0.0402	0.2615

In the last column we find the calculated F-values that have been included in Table V.12. The critical F-value is in this case

$$F_{0.05}(m, T-k-m+1) = F(2, 13) = 3.81$$

since the number of observations $T=17$ and there are $k=3$ explanatory variables.

Since no suitable teststatistic on autocorrelation is available yet, in case of more equations we do not test on autocorrelation. This means that model $QY[Q_{-1}\ Y_{-1}\ c]$ is accepted here without any test whatsoever. Model $QY[Q_{-1}\ c]$ is not admitted on the ground of the calculated F-value of 927.59. Consequently, the data for this model have not been computed. This has been done, however, for the models $QY[Q_{-1}\ Y_{-1}]$ and $QY[Y_{-1}\ c]$. On the ground of the results obtained for the latter model neither $QY[Q_{-1}]$ nor $QY[c]$ appears to be admitted. The tests-statistic of $QY[Y_{-1}]$ has not been calculated. It is already clear before-hand, that Y_{-1} may not be omitted. All 4 admitted models prove to be relevant. According to Lemma 5 the forecasting interval of model $QY[Q_{-1}\ Y_{-1}\ c]$ is obviously larger than the one of $QY[Q_{-1}\ Y_{-1}]$ when the computed F-value for the elimination of the constant is smaller than the critical value.

$$\left[1 - \frac{1}{T-k-m+1}\right]^{m} - 1 = \left[1 + \frac{1}{13}\right]^{2} - 1 = 0.16\,.$$

None of the 4 models has an F-value below F_0. The choice from the relevant and admitted models is determined by the value of $\det \theta\hat{\Omega}$. For model $QY[Y_{-1}]$ we get

$$S = \frac{E'E}{T-k} = \begin{bmatrix} 0.8653 & -0.7420 \\ -0.7420 & 2.2159 \end{bmatrix}.$$

Then, according to (4.2) we have

$$\hat{\Omega} = (1 + q)\, S = \begin{bmatrix} 1.0520 & -0.9021 \\ -0.9021 & 2.6941 \end{bmatrix}.$$

In this $q = Y_t^2 / \Sigma Y_{t-1}^2$ has the same value as in the models $Y[Y_{-1}]$ and $Q[Y_{-1}]$. The diagonal elements of the matrix $\hat{\Omega}$ were indeed already known from the 2 models mentioned. The covariances, however, are new. The value of θ changes too. It becomes – see (3.41) –

$$\theta = \frac{(T-k)\,m}{T-k-m+1} F_\alpha(m, T-k-m+1)$$

$$= \tfrac{32}{15} \times F_{0.05}(2.15) = \tfrac{32}{15} \times 3.68 = 7.8507\,.$$

Hence $\det \theta\hat{\Omega} = 124.5238$ (billions of guilders)^2 or $\sqrt{\det \theta\hat{\Omega}} = 7.8507 \sqrt{\det \hat{\Omega}} = 11.1590$ billions of guilders. For the models $QY[Q_{-1}\ Y_{-1}\ c]$ and $QY[Y_{-1}\ c]$ we get for $\sqrt{\det \theta\hat{\Omega}}$ respectively 14.6420 and 14.6680 billions of guilders. We are more complete for model $QY[Q_{-1}\ Y_{-1}]$, viz.

$$S = \begin{bmatrix} 0.7496 & -0.6962 \\ -0.6962 & 2.3113 \end{bmatrix}$$

$$q = 0.2279$$

$$\hat{\Omega} = \begin{bmatrix} 0.9203 & -0.8549 \\ -0.8549 & 2.8380 \end{bmatrix}$$

$$\theta = 8.0143$$

$$\det \theta\hat{\Omega} = 120.8120 \quad \text{billions}^2 \text{ of guilders}$$

$$\sqrt{\det \theta\hat{\Omega}} = 10.9914 \quad \text{billions of guilders}.$$

This means that from the 4 admitted and relevant models model $QY[Q_{-1}\ Y_{-1}]$ has the smallest unweighted forecasting interval for 1966. If one determines weighingcoefficients for the variances of the forecasting errors, $QY[Q_{-1}\ Y_{-1}]$ remains preferable as long as

$$w_Y < 0.79 w_Q$$

or, with the weighingcoefficients on the basis of the standard deviations

$$w_Y < 2.01 w_Q$$

These inequality relations are rather far apart. If we stick to the latter, this implies that model $QY[Q_{-1} \ \ Y_{-1}]$ is preferable to $QY[Y_{-1}]$ as long as one is of the opinion that damage caused by an error in the forecast of Y_t is smaller than twice the damage that is caused by an error in the forecast of $\mathbf{Q}_t$. This is more difficult to evaluate than in the case of a simultaneous forecast of 2 years. However, it seems as if on short term a forecasting error in $\mathbf{Q}_t$ does not cause more than twice as much damage as an error in the forecast of $\mathbf{Y}_t$. If model $QY[Q_{-1} \ \ Y_{-1}]$ is chosen the forecasting procedure is

$$\hat{Q} = 0.3949 Q_{-1} + 0.00738 Y_{-1}$$

$$\hat{Y} = -\,0.2169 Q_{-1} + 1.0994 Y_{-1}$$

in which the coefficients are obtained from a regression according to least squares of Q and Y on Q_{-1} and Y_{-1}.

The pointestimates are

$$\hat{Q} = 610 \text{ millions of guilders}$$

$$\hat{Y} = 75.79 \text{ billions of guilders}.$$

This result differs from the forecasts given earlier for 1966 because:

(1) Less information has been used: $\tilde{w}_{-1}$ has not been considered.

(2) There have only been selections with columns. We shall return to this.

(3) The simultaneous forecast imposes certain obligations that lead to larger intervals for the separate variables. This is an implication of Lemma 2.

The 95% forecasting interval of model $QY[Q_{-1} \ \ Y_{-1}]$ is represented by the inequality

$$\mathbf{e}_t' \hat{\Omega}_{-1} \mathbf{e}_t \leqslant \theta$$

or

$$[\mathbf{e}_Q \, \mathbf{e}_Y] \begin{bmatrix} 1.5087 & 0.4545 \\ 0.4545 & 0.4893 \end{bmatrix} \begin{bmatrix} \mathbf{e}_Q \\ \mathbf{e}_Y \end{bmatrix} \leqslant 8.0143 .$$

See Figure V.2.

95% CONFIDENCE INTERVAL OF MODEL
YQ [$Q_{-1}Y_{-1}$] (billions of guilders)

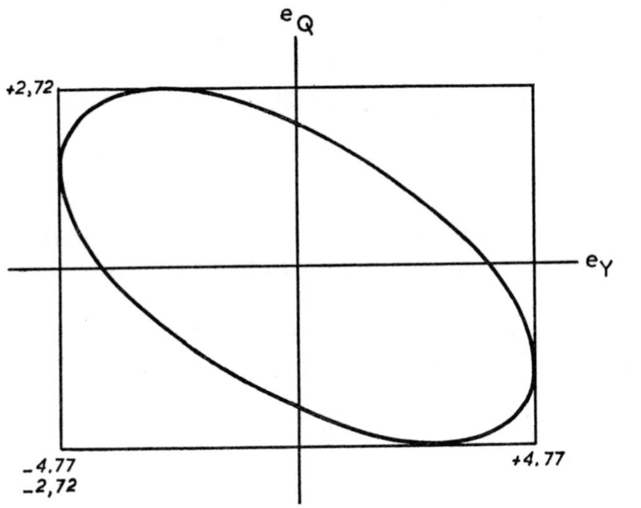

Fig. V.2.

The area of the ellipse constituted the basis for the selection. None of the other admitted models has a forecasting area smaller than the one of model $QY[Q_{-1} \;\; Y_{-1}]$. It is

$$(\pi\theta)^{m/2} \sqrt{\det \hat{\Omega}} = 10.99\,\pi\,.$$

Giving forecasting ellipses is not very useful in practical discussions and ministerial memoranda. If the number of variables that is to be forecasted is larger than 2, a graphical presentation is even out of the question. Hymans (1969) proposed, therefore, to take the supporting hyperplanes as a basis for the presentation[13]. This means a presentation for each equation, as if the latter were not part of a simultaneous model. We get

$$\hat{Q}_{66} = \hat{Q} \pm \sqrt{\theta s_Q^2 (1 + q)}$$

$$\hat{Y}_{66} = \hat{Y} \pm \sqrt{\theta s_Y^2 (1 + q)}\,.$$

This gives for the optimal model

$$Q_{66} = 0.61 \pm \sqrt{0.9203 \times 8.0143}$$
$$Y_{66} = 75.79 \pm \sqrt{2.8380 \times 8.0143}$$

or

$$-2110 \leqslant Q_{66} \leqslant 3330 \text{ millions of guilders}$$
$$71.02 \leqslant Y_{66} \leqslant 80.56 \text{ billions of guilders}.$$

In Figure V.2 the bounds are presented by the rectangle written around the ellipse. The intervals can easily be read from the graph, when the origin of the system of coordinates is removed to the pointestimation of Y_t and Q_t.

It remains to be seen whether the model $YQ[Q_{-1} \;\; Y_{-1}]$ can still be improved by considering the following alternative

$$Q_t = Q_{t-1} + \qquad + \mathbf{u}_{1t}$$
$$Y_t = \qquad Y_{t-1} + \mathbf{u}_{2t}$$

This model is derived from $QY[Q_{-1} \;\; Y_{-1}]$ when in both equations one coefficient is set equal to 0. This model seems to be preferable, because we preferred $Q[Q_{-1}]$ over $Y[Q_{-1} \;\; Y_{-1}]$ and $Y[Y_{-1}]$ over $Y[Q_{-1} \;\; Y_{-1}]$. In the latter case the relative standard error of the coefficient belonging to Q_{-1} was so large that $Y[Q_{-1} \;\; Y_{-1}]$ was not even relevant.

Although there is every reason to try out the latter model, the problems here are such that the model has not been taken into consideration. For, in the first place least squares does not give the optimal forecasting procedure here. Zellner (1962) shows that knowledge about the zerocoefficients in a reduced form creates possibilities for a more efficient estimation of the reduced form coefficients, namely through

$$P^* = [X'S^{-1}X]^{-1} X'S^{-1}Y$$

in which S is the efficient estimate of Σ, mentioned before. Zellner demonstrates that the characteristics of P^* asymptotically do not differ from those of P. It must still be proved whether P^*X_t is also the optimal forecasting procedure in such a situation, but also whether $P^{*\prime}_{.i}(rE'E^*)^{-1}P^*_{.i}$ has still an F-distribution. It has not if the number of explanatory variables of the various equations is not equal. To this problem hardly any attention has been paid in the literature.

NOTES TO CHAPTER V

1 $Q_t \simeq N(0, \sigma^2)$ has not been considered as a model.

2 Recently a new computerprogram was conceived by F. A. G. den Butter. With this program we made an analysis starting from 2 maximum-specifications of 8 explanatory variables. The first contained all explanators used in this chapter apart from B_{-1} and M_{-1}. The second contained all but Q_{-1} and t^3. More information is given in Appendix A.

3 Defined as the magnitude, mentioned in "National Accounts 1967", C.B.S. (1967), p. 112, Table 47, line 3 and line 6, line 15, line 18.

4 As indicated in the table the figures for 1965 appeared to be not yet final in the source mentioned. However, the difference is only slight.

5 And smaller than the value $4 - d_L$, which has not been indicated in the table.

6 Also $Q[t^3 \; t^2 \; c]$ has in Table V.2 two coefficients that are significantly different from 0. But setting both coefficients simultaneously equal to zero results in $Q[c]$, a model that is not admitted on other grounds. However, according to the procedure in point (5) on page 71 this simultaneous test is carried out together with other simultaneous tests on $Q[c]$ derived from $Q[t^2 \; t \; c]$ and $Q[t^3 \; t \; c]$, as long as $Q[c]$ is admitted.

7 See note 6 on page 97.

8 Based on the forecasting intervals for the separate years. These intervals form also the basis for the publication of simultaneous intervals. See Section 5.5 about this.

9 If $Q[c]$ in Table V.6 would be admitted, it would still have been eliminated on behalf of Table V.2. So in an actual investigation one should check before calculating the intervals whether the models involved have not proved to be inadmissible in any group. (See Subsection 4.3.2, ad 4).

10 See e.g. Orcutt and Winokur (1969).

11 With $s^2 = .3825$, $q = .00327$ and $F(1.34) = 4.13$ even an interval of 2518 million which is smaller than all intervals of Table V.10.

12 In Figure V.1 the interval has been indicated as a constant area between 2 parallel lines instead of a changing area, dependent on Q_{-1} and $\tilde{w}_{-1}$.

13 See note 6 on page 46.

APPENDIX A

Recently a new computerprogram in Algol was conceived by F. A. G. den Butter. With this program an analysis was made starting from the following two *maximumspecifications* with 8 explanatory variables each:

$$Q\,[Q_{-1}\;\; Q_{-2}\;\; c\;\; t\;\; t^2\;\; t^3\;\; Y_{-1}\;\; \tilde{w}_{-1}] \tag{1}$$

and

$$Q\,[\qquad Q_{-2}\;\; c\;\; t\;\; t^2\qquad Y_{-1}\;\; \tilde{w}_{-1}\;\; B_{-1}\;\; M_{-1}]. \tag{2}$$

Both can be derived from the following model

$$\begin{aligned} &Y_t = X_t + B_t - M_t \\ &M_t - \delta_M M_{t-1} = \mu_1 Y_t + \mu_2 Y_{t-1} \\ &B_t - \delta_B B_{t-1} = v_0 + v_1 t + v_2 t^2 + v_3 t^3 \\ &X_t = \xi_0 + \xi_1 Y_{t-1} + \xi_2 \tilde{w}_{t-1} \end{aligned} \tag{3}$$

in which the symbols represent the same variables as in Chapter V (see Table V.1).

If $\delta_M = \delta_B$ (3) leads to the reduced form Equation (1).

If $\delta_M \neq \delta_B$ and $v_3 = 0$ we end up with (2).

AI. THE PROGRAM

The computerprogram consists of two parts. (We use the definitions of Subsections 4.4.3 and 4.3.3.)

1. *The Construction of the Set $\mathscr{R}$*

Indications are given why particular models from the set of all models considered were not included in $\mathscr{R}$. In part 1 the testprocedures are carried out according to the 10 points in Subsection 4.3.3. So simultaneous tests on groups of coefficients are included.

2. *The Selection of the Forecasting Procedure*

A concise survey is given of the indicators of the models contained in $\mathscr{R}$. The models are ranked in decreasing order of their forecasting intervals.

AII. THE RESULTS FOR (1) AND (2)

Table AI gives a survey of the results of the calculations for (1) and (2), both generating $2^8-1=255$ models.

TABLE AI

Survey of the sets $\mathscr{R}$ attached to maximum specification (1) and (2)

	(1)	(2)
Total number of models considered	255	255
Number of models calculated	65	86
Number of models in $\mathscr{R}$	27	27
among which:		
with 1 explanatory variable	1	–
with 2 explanatory variables	–	–
with 3 explanatory variables	3	5
with 4 explanatory variables	11	14
with 5 explanatory variables	9	7
with 6 explanatory variables	3	1

With respect to (1) it appeared that $\mathscr{R}$ contained 12 models with 5 or 6 explanatory variables. These models were not considered in Chapter V. In the latter chapter only 1 specification of 4 variables was considered (see Table V.5). This specification is referred to N when we start from (1). The 3 models with 3 explanatory variables in the table above were not considered in Chapter V. The model $Q[Y_{-1}]$ was included in that chapter. It is also here when we start from (1.)

The best model in Chapter V was $Q[Q_{-1}\ w_{-1}]$. It is not admitted here. The best model is $Q[t,\ c,\ w_{-1}]$ having an interval of 3760 millions of guilders for 1966.

When starting from (2) none of the models of Chapter V are admitted. The model $Q[t,\ c,\ \tilde{w}_{-1}]$ considered above was also here included in $\mathscr{R}$. It ranked fifth. The best model was $Q[Q_{-2}\ Y_{-1}\ B_{-1}\ \tilde{w}_{-1}]$ with an interval of 3369 millions of guilders. It appeared that there were no great differences between the widths of the intervals of the 2 sets $\mathscr{R}$. The level of (1) was roughly 4400 millions of guilders, as compared to 4000 millions for (2).

For both maximumspecifications the program used 57 millihours on an Electrologica X8, including compilation of the program. To evaluate computer time needed, we added the variable Q_{-1} to maximumspecification (2), introducing not only $2^9-2^8=256$ new models, but also exact multicollinearity. The program used 71 millihours, 243 models were calculated. The set $\mathscr{R}$ contained 57 models. It was somehow remarkable that $Q[Q_{-2}\ Y_{-1}\ B_{-1}\ \tilde{w}_{-1}]$ that was for 1966 the best model derived from (2) also ranked first in this maximumspecification of 9 explanatory variables.

BIBLIOGRAPHY

Abbreviations used in the Bibliography

A.M.S.	Annals of Mathematical Statistics.
B.	Biometrika.
E.	Econometrica.
J.A.S.A.	Journal of the American Statistical Association.
J.R.S.S.	Journal of the Royal Statistical Society.
R.I.S.I.	Review of the International Statistical Institute.
S.N.	Statistica Neerlandica.
C.P.B.	Central Planning Bureau, The Hague.
N.E.H.	Netherlands School of Economics, Rotterdam.

Abrahamse, A. P. J. and Koerts, J., 'New Estimators of Disturbances in Regression Analysis', J.A.S.A. **66** (1971) 71–74.

Allen, R. G. D., *Macro-Economic Theory*, McMillan, London, 1967.

Anderson, T. W., *An Introduction to Multivariate Statistical Analysis*, Wiley, New York, 1958.

Barten, A. P., 'Note on Unbiased Estimation of the Squared Multiple Correlation Coefficient, *S.N.* **16** (1962), 151–163.

Beld, C. A. van den, 'An Experimental Medium-Term Macromodel for the Dutch Economy', in *Mathematical Model Building in Economics and Industry*, C. Griffith and Cy, London, 1968.

Beld, C. A. van den and Russchen, A., *Forecast and Realisation. The Forecasts by the Netherlands Central Planning Bureau 1953–1963*, C.P.B. Monograph No. 10, Staatsdrukkerij, The Hague, 1965.

Bertels, C. P. and Nauta, D., *Inleiding tot het modelbegrip*, W. de Haan, Bussum, 1969.

Bradu, D. and Mundlak, Y., 'Estimation in Lognormal Linear Models', *J.A.S.A.* **65** (1970), 198–211.

Butter, F. A. G. den, 'Two Years', fortcoming article.

Centraal Planbureau, *Centraal Economisch Plan, 1960–1971*, Staatsdrukkerij, 's-Gravenhage, each year.

Christ, C. F., *Econometric Models and Methods*, Wiley, New York, 1966.

Cox, D. R., 'Prediction by Exponentially Weighted Moving Averages and Related Methods', *J.R.S.S.*, Series B**23**, (1961), 414–424.

Cramér, H., *Mathematical Methods of Statistics*, Princeton University Press, Princeton, 1946.

Cramer, J. S., *Empirical Econometrics*, North-Holland Publishing Co., Amsterdam, 1969.

Duesenberry, J. S., Eckstein, O., and Fromm, G., 'A Simulation of the United States in Recession', *E.* **28** (1960), 749–809.

Durbin, J., 'The Fitting of Time-series Models', *R.I.S.I.* **28** (1960), 233–243.

Durbin, J., 'Testing for Serial Correlation in Least Squares Regression when Some of the Regressors are Lagged Dependent Variables', *E.* **38** (1970), 410–421.

Durbin, J. and Watson, G. S., 'Testing for Serial Correlation in Least Squares Regression I', *B.* **37** (1950), 409–428.

Durbin, J. and Watson, G. S., 'Testing for Serial Correlation in Least Squares Regression, II', *B.* **38** (1951), 159–178.

Feldstein, M. S., 'The Error of Forecast in Econometric Models when the Forecast-Period Exogeneous Variables are Stochastic', *E.* **39** (1971), 55–60.

Glejser, H., 'A New Test for Heteroskedasticity', *J.A.S.A.* **64** (1969), 316–323.

Goldberger, A. S., *Econometric Theory*, Wiley, New York, 1964.

Goldberger, A. S., Nagar, A. L., and Odeh, H. S., 'The Covariance Matrices of Reduced-Form Coefficients of Forecasts for a Structural Economic Model', *E.* **29** (1961), 556–573.

Goldfeld, S. M. and Quandt, R. E., 'Some Tests for Homoscedasticity', *J.A.S.A.* **60** (1965) 539–547.

Graybill, F. A., *An Introduction to Linear Statistical Models*, Vol. 1, McGraw Hill, New York, 1961.

Hart, B. I., 'Significance Levels for the Ratio of the Mean Square Successive Difference to the Variance', *A.M.S.* **13** (1942), 445–447.

Hemelrijk, J., 'Underlining Random Variables', *S.N.* **20** (1966), 1–7.

Hooper, J. W. and Zellner, A., 'The Error of Forecast for Multivariate Regression Models, *E.* **29** (1961), 544–555.

Hurwicz, L., 'Least Square Bias in Time-Series', Chapter XV of Koopmans, 1950.

Hymans, S. E., 'Simultaneous Confidence Intervals in Econometric Forecasting', *E.* **36** (1968) 18–30.

Kramer, G., 'On the Durbin-Watson Bounds Test in the Case of Regression through the Origin', report presented to the Fourth 'Winter Seminar' of the Econometric Society, Hamburg 1970.

Klein, L. R., *Economic Fluctuations in the United States 1921–1941*, Wiley, New York, 1950.

Klein, L. R. and Goldberger, A. S., *An Econometric Model of the United States 1929–1959*, North-Holland Publishing Co., Amsterdam, 1955.

Koerts, J. and Abrahamse, A. P. J., *On the Theory and Application of the General Linear Model*, Rotterdam University Press, Rotterdam, 1969.

Koopmans, T. C., *Statistical Inference in Dynamic Economic Models*, Wiley, New York, 1950.

Kooyman, J. and Merkies, A. H. Q. M., 'Possible Growth in the Netherlands up to 1985', in *Long-Term Planning UN Publication*, New York 1971, C.P.B. reprint No. 1/1972.

Liu, T. C., 'Underidentification, Structural Estimation and Forecasting', *E.* **28** (1960), 855–865.

Malinvaud, E, *Statistical Methods of Econometrics*, North-Holland Publishing Co., Amsterdam, 1968.

Malinvaud, E., 'Estimation et prévision dans les modèles économiques autorégressifs', *R.I.S.I.* **29** (2) (1961), 1–32.

Mann, H. B. and Wald, A., 'On the Statistical Treatment of Linear Stochastic Difference Equations, *E.* **11** (1943), 173–220.

Marriott, F. H. C. and Pope, J., 'Bias in the Estimation of Auto-correlations', *B* **41** (1954), 393–403.

Mirsky, L., *An Introduction to Linear Algebra*, Clarendon Press, Oxford, 1955.

Neudecker, H., 'The Kronecker Matrix Product and some of its Applications in Econometrics, *S.N.* **22** (1968), 69–82.

Neyman, J. and Pearson, E. S., 'On the Use and the Interpretation of Certain Test Criteria for the Purposes of Statistical Inference, Part 1', in *Statistical Papers of J. Neyman and E. S. Pearson*, University Press, Cambridge, 1967.

Orcutt, G. H. and Cockrane, D., 'A Sampling Study of the Merits of the Autoregressive and Reduced form Transformations in Regression Analysis', *J.A.S.A.* **44** (1949), 356–372.

Orcutt, G. H. and Winokur, H. S., Jr., 'First Order Autoregression: Interference, Estimation and Prediction', *E.* **37** (1969), 1–14.

Pearson, E. S. and Hartley, H. O., *Biometrika Tables for Statisticians*, Vol. 1 (3rd ed.), Cambridge University Press, Cambridge, 1966.

Quenouille, M. H., 'Approximate Tests of Correlation in Time Series', *J.R.S.S.*, Series B**11** (1949), 68–83.

Rao, P. and Griliches, Z., 'Small Sample Properties of Several Two-Stage Regression Methods in the Context of Auto-Correlated Errors', *J.A.S.A.* **64** (1969), 253–272.

Rubin, H., 'Consistency of Maximum-Likelihood Estimates in the Explosive Case', Chapter XIV of Koopmans, 1950.

Sandee, J., 'Schatten, toetsen en beslissen in de macro-economie', *De Economist* **114** (1966), 473–484.

Shenton, L. R. and Johnson, W. L., 'Moments of a Serial Correlation Coefficient', *J.R.S.S.*, Series B**27**, (1965), 308–320.

Somermeyer, W. H., 'Specificatie van Economische Relaties', *De Economist* **115** (1967), 1–26.

Stekler, H. O., 'Forecasting with Econometric Models: An Evaluation', *E.* **36** (1968), 437–463.

Theil, H., 'Who Forecasts Best?', *International Economic Papers*, No. 5 (1955).

Theil, H., *Economic Forecasts and Policy*, 2nd ed. (1st ed. 1958), North-Holland Publishing Co., Amsterdam, 1965.

Theil, H., *Principles of Econometrics*, North-Holland Publishing Co., Amsterdam, 1971.

Tinbergen, J., *Economic Policy: Principles and Design*, North-Holland Publishing Co., Amsterdam, 1956.

Verdoorn, P. J. and Eijk, C. J. van, 'Experimental Short-Term Forecasting Models', Document for the 20th meeting of the Econometric Society at Bilbao 1958, mimeographed.

Verdoorn, P. J. and Post, J. J., 'Capacity and the Short-Term Multipliers', Document for the 16th symposium of the Colston Research Society at Bristol, *Colston Papers* **16**, C.P.B. reprint No. 92 (1964).

Vereniging voor Economie, 10e Vlaamse wetenschappelijk economisch congres, *De behoeften van de mens en de Belgische economie in de jaren tachtig*, Centrum voor Econometrie en Management Sciences, Vrije Universiteit, Brussel, 1971.

Werf, D. van der, 'De westduitse economie in vijftien vergelijkingen', Ph. D. thesis, Amsterdam 1971.

Wiener, N., *Extrapolation, Interpolation and Smoothing of Stationary Time Series*, Wiley, New York, 1949.

Wilks, S. S., 'Certain Generalisations in the Analysis of Variance', *B.* **24** (1932), 471–494.

Winkel, E. G. F. van and Fraser, D. J., *Tijdreeksvoorspellingen en hun bewaking*, Samsom, Alphen a/d Rijn, 1970.

Wonnacott, J. and Wonnacott, T. H., *Econometrics*, Wiley, New York, 1970.

Zellner, A., 'An Efficient Method of Estimating Seemingly Unrelated Regressions and Tests for Aggregation Bias', *J.A.S.A.* **57** (1962), 348–368.